Paterson of Cyrene

A Biography

by

David A.C. Walker

MAMBO PRESS
Gweru, P.O. Box 779
Harare, P. Bag 66002, Kopje
Gokomere, P. Bag 9213, Masvingo

ISBN   0 86922 340 2

Printed and published in Zimbabwe
by Mambo Press, Senga Road, Gweru
1985

CONTENTS

Preface and Acknowledgements

Ned Paterson was one of the great characters of central Africa. He was a cheerful eccentric, a mischievous clergyman with a salty wit who loved to startle people and played outrageous practical jokes. He was a comic cleric who showed the world a happy Christ of love and gentle laughter. In addition he helped unleash the flood of modern Zimbabwean art, by teaching and encouragement.

The arts, he wrote, express the hopes and aspiration of people. He saw how great is the human need for loving appreciation, how easy it is to censure and hurt. The God of love is one who appreciates and enjoys us despite our faults. We serve Him by encouraging and taking joy in the work of one another. We bring His love to one another by encouragement, praise and caring.

Priest, artist, archaeologist, linguist, teacher, writer and family man, Paterson was a young man all his life. He brought into it gaiety, energy, enthusiasm, integrity, and love of God and men, women and children. He knew the child in us never dies. We all need at times to fool around a bit, for part of us is a child all our days. He enjoyed clowning himself, and if he seemed at times ludicrous, he did not mind so long as his clowning gave others a bit of fun. A friendly kiss for a majestic, world-weary matron, or a cheerful smile at a wedding or a funeral helped the sun shine a little brighter. He would have loved the laughter at his own funeral.

He won the love of all sorts of people by his cheerful simplicity of life. He accepted people for what they were, and accepted himself. He knew he had many faults, but accepted them and lived with them. He did not make claims for himself or try to live selfishly at the cost of others. He did not thrust forward but was content to be himself; to live cheaply and honestly. He did not envy others' wealth or happiness but lived simply within his means and built up the self-respect of the people he met. He loved to make people laugh. Even in old age, blind and in a lot of pain, 'he always had a twinkle in his eye'. He was one of the most successful of his profession in inspiring local people to become priests and join him in the service of his Master.

What made Paterson the man he was? His Scottish poverty and close family taught him to value love and religion. The nearness of death in his childhood taught him not to fear it nor to place much value on possessions. He had a gift of caricature which was fortunately encouraged, and firm parents who taught him to value time. His mother once said 'What have I done that God gave me a mad son?' and there was one way in which she certainly had made him odd man out in the family. The Patersons were almost as fervent Scots as they were Christians. Ned's parents named his brothers James, Douglas, Leslie and Gordon — great old Scottish royal and noble names, from royalty, six earldoms, a duchy, and a marquisate. But in 1895, when he was born, the line of Queen Victoria had just been further secured through the birth of Prince Edward (VIII) to Prince Edward (VII)'s son George (V). Ned was given the English names Edward and George. He retained a fierce antipathy to the British monarchy till he met George VI's Scottish queen Elizabeth, later a valued ally of the arts of Central Africa especially Zimbabwe.

A book on Ned was first proposed about 1953. In 1972 the Rev R. Hambrook of USPG drafted a manuscript but died soon after. About 1980 the draft was brought back to Zimbabwe and a year or two later I was invited by Ned's widow, now Mrs Kathleen Garrs, to write a completely new biography making use of the Hambrook manuscript and many other sources.

My particular gratitude is due to Mrs Kathleen Garrs; to Mrs Mary Ball, Ned's eldest daughter; to their husbands, Jack Garrs and Barrie Ball; to Lady Violet le Gros Clark who lent me many marvellous letters; to Fr Albert Plangger and Lady Margaret Tredgold without whose driving energy and enthusiasm the project might never have been completed; to Canons R.A. Ewbank and R.H. Clark; to the late Douglas Paterson (Ned's brother); Ned's former pupils and students; and to the loving memories of Fr Reginald Hambrook and Dr Nicholas Paterson whose short life shone with the brilliance of a loving star.

In addition I am grateful for assistance and suggestions to the following institutions and people:

The Directors, Principals, Librarians and staffs of:
The Central School of Arts and Crafts;
Gweru Memorial Library;
Mambo Press, Gweru; Mkoba Teachers' College;
Mzilikazi Art Centre; the National Archives of Zimbabwe;
the National Arts Foundation;
the National Gallery of Zimbabwe;
St Paul's Theological College, Grahamstown;
the United Society for the Propagation of the Gospel;
the University of Zimbabwe;
and in particular the members of the Canon Paterson Craft Centre in Mbare.

Among the many individuals consulted the following have been particularly helpful:

Bill Arnold, Mrs P. Battigelli, Mrs G.K. Bliss, Noel Brettell, Bernard Cairns, Bernard Chiadzwa, Mrs Ellen Chudy, Canon J. Fenwick, Mrs L. Frangcon-Jones, Mr & Mrs Hugh Finn, Mrs Barbara Gibbs, Sir Humphrey and Dame Molly Gibbs; Canon R.H. Grinham, Mrs Phyllis Hiller; Burford Hurry, Mrs Vivienne Jedeikin, Job Kekana, Morris Kestelman, Bishop Robert Mercer, Mr & Mrs Morris Mills, Mrs D. Moony, Rev Dewi Morgan, Joseph Muli, Barnabas Ndudzo, Mrs Patricia Nisbet, Rev Stanley Nyahwa, Fr Neil Pierce, Rob Prentice, W. Roberts who first introduced me to Ned's work, Canon Chris Ross, Mr & Mrs G. Scully, R. Cherer Smith, Sam Songo, Paul Sykes, Miss Barbara Tredgold, Lawrence Vambe, Miss K. Walker, Fr T. Wardle and Fr S.P. Woodfield.

There were many others too numerous to mention.

As this is perhaps my first publication, my gratitude is recorded to my parents. May they live long enough to see this work in print and to enjoy it.

Introduction

Art education in schools before the late nineteenth century was largely used to train manual dexterity in copying from usually geometrical models. There was very little training in specifically artistic skills. Artists and craftsmen learned from their professional superiors and peers, and the traditional training for an artist was to assist and learn from an artist of established reputation. Formal training in art, even in England, was geared to the requirements of the students' society, and in British society art held a law status. The copying skills that were taught in general were those which were of potential value, the basis for design and perception skills needed for industry. Such art as was taught in the colonies also reflected these values. Local traditions were totally ignored and art, if taught at all, consisted merely of learning to copy from geometrical forms or sometimes pictures.

From 1860 onwards, however, under John Ruskin's influence, there was increasing emphasis on pictorial composition and on the training of perception through the detailed observation of forms in nature. From 1874 Friedrich Froebel's ideas were spread in Britain through the Training College at Stockwell in London. Froebel saw spontaneous imaginative artistic expression as a means of self-development for the child. In 1899 a new British syllabus laid some stress on children's drawing from memory, thereby sifting out irrelevant detail, and choosing their own subjects. In the 1920s, under the influence of the Austrian Franz Cizek, the British artist Roger Fry, and the teacher Marion Richardson, there was increasing encouragement of spontaneous artistic expression among British children.

Interest in traditional African art had developed by this time. An increasing number of modern artists such as Picasso found inspiration in early African, American and Polynesian masks and artifacts. In 1910 and 1912 Roger Fry held two exhibitions in London of art by the new French and English painters, who like Cizek held that art should express the feelings of the artist. African art also influenced the Cubists in their desire to reduce contours to simple lines and masses, a tendency still apparent in Zimbabwean stone sculpture.

By the 1920s also British official attitudes towards the colonies had undergone a change. The complacent assumption of imperial power had received severe blows from the Anglo-Boer and First World Wars, and increasingly civil servants realized the potential value of the traditional crafts. Already in countries like Nigeria and Ghana the 'educated' black who despised his own culture and people was a source for concern.

In 1922 Aino Onabolu, a Yoruba Chief, became his country's first school art teacher, and began a life-long campaign to have art taught in all Nigerian schools. He succeeded in 1927 in having K.C. Murray appointed as an Education Officer in this area. Murray learned and taught the traditional craft techniques and tried to establish a syllabus in art despite great government opposition.

In 1925 Achimota College in Ghana started with Dr J. Aggrey, a black, as Vice-Principal. Dr Aggrey wanted to see art taught there, and in 1927 George Stevens became the art teacher. Stevens was concerned with the gap between formal art training in the Western style and the African traditions.

He found his students drew scurrilous cartoons for their amusement, and encouraged them to draw scenes expressed in terms of contemporary life, and landscapes in their official art classes. Stevens and Murray held London exhibitions of their students' work in 1929 and 1937 respectively, and in the late 1930s H.V. Meyerowitz and a team of British artists and craftsmen built up at Achimota a syllabus blending Western and traditional craft methods.

In 1935 J.P. Greenlaw joined a teachers training college at Bakht in the Sudan and set up art teaching there. In 1936 Margaret Trowell started an art group for youths in Uganda, and their work was shown in London in 1939. Her art group evolved under her tremendous enthusiasm into the Makerere School of Fine Art, training artists and teachers. She based her work as a starting point on the traditional craft designs and patterns of the region, and led from this to pictorial work. One force which drove her on was her fear that the spiritual life expressed in African art might be submerged for generations under western materialism. (Article in *Oversea Education*, Jan 1936, cit Carline p. 181.)

Paterson left Cyrene in 1953 and moved to Harare where he taught in several schools and art centres until his death in 1974. He was also a member of the Board of the National Gallery. He had by his encouragement helped to pave the foundations for a modern Zimbabwean tradition in art.

Paterson's own artistic work included drawings, posters, wood-carving, and work in bronze, silver and pottery. Most of his major work was in church decoration, including internal decoration of Johannesburg Anglican Cathedral and many other churches, fresco work on Cyrene Mission Chapel, and the huge suspended Cross in enamelled perspex and aluminium in Marondera Anglican Church.

Contemporaries of Paterson included Sister Pauline, C.R. who taught bas-relief religious carving at St Faith's Mission from 1939 to her death in 1954, often using designs provided by Paterson, and Fr John Groeber, who came to this country from Switzerland in 1939. Fr Groeber first taught art at Silveira Mission, Bikita, and in 1948 went to build up a new Mission at Serima. The art he fostered was African in manner but Christian in subject. He introduced his boys to Congolese and West African masks. Their economy of detail and contour, clearly defined planes and cubes, and play of shapes, gives each a rhythm of its own. The Serima style stresses the vulnerability and dignity of man through the use of wood or stone reduced to a series of planes, usually outlined with fine lines.

Elsewhere in Africa art developed after the War, with varying degrees of success.

In Nigeria Fr Kevin Carroll fostered the local traditional style of woodcarving on Christian themes, and Michael Cardew taught pottery. At Ndaleni in Natal sculptures, murals and mosaics were produced, from traditional, found and improvised materials. Art schools were founded at Brazzaville and Leopoldville in the Congo, and in Ethiopia. Several schools were founded around 1958. In 1959 Malangatana Valente began his career in Mozambique.

In 1957 the National Gallery in Harare was set up and formally opened by H.M. the Queen Mother, who had taken a great interest in Paterson's work. Other dominant influences were the Gallery's Chairman, Sir Stephen Courtauld, a cultured benefactor of the arts, and its Director, Frank McEwen. The Gallery was viewed as a focal point for the arts in the Federation of Rhodesia and Nyasaland and McEwen had built up by 1961 a community of artists there which has become known as the Workshop School. He hoped to get blacks and whites to work together, an exercise in racial harmony, but found the interests of the two groups were too different. In 1962 an International Congress of African Culture was held at the Gallery, with nearly 400 exhibits illustrating both traditional and modern African art and European art under African influence. 10 of the works were by former students of Paterson. Exhibitions of work by local artists were also put on in London in 1963, 1965, 1969, and 1972, and Paris in 1970 and 1971.

With the 1960s and the independence of many states, art flourished. Big cultural clubs such as the Mbaris in Nigeria (1961 – 63) and Chemechemi in Nairobi (1963) developed arts for the people, including drama, music, dance and so on which cannot be wholly separated from the static visual arts as in the West.

Paterson had seen his need to view the arts holistically at Cyrene as early as 1949, and Sir Stephen Courtauld had seen the National Gallery as the future centre of a cultural complex involving theatre and music.

U.D.I. affected the Workshop School in various ways. A shortage of imported artists' materials encouraged the School to move towards sculpture in serpentine stone and away from paint. It also stimulated the formation of other artists groups, notably Tom Blomefield's Tengenenge sculptors and a group at Vukutu Farm in Inyanga, first under McEwen and later under W. Burdett-Coutts. Mrs Pat Pearce encouraged rural craftwork mainly in Inyanga and the Eastern Districts. Art teaching in the country as a whole however remained limited. There was some art taught in Primary and in White Secondary schools, mainly for examinations. Paterson had his big art classes in Harare and art continued spasmodically at Cyrene. Carving and pottery were also taught from 1963 at Mzilikazi Art Centre in Bulawayo by Janine Mackenzie and others, while Paterson's former pupils and a small group such as Barnabas Ndudzo taught by Job Kekana took pupils in the traditional way. Other teaching artists included the painter John Hlatywayo and the metal work sculptor Arthur Azevedo. Art was also taught by the Catholic Church at Driefontein Mission, with an emphasis on religious woodcarving in the tradition established by Fr Groeber.

The war inhibited efforts by the National Gallery to stimulate imaginative art in local schools, though it was taught at Hillside Teachers' College (then restricted to Whites), Mkoba Teachers' College, and United College of Education; also latterly, at Mutare and Seki Teachers' Colleges, and elsewhere since the war.

Costs have so far (1984), prevented a general Secondary School syllabus from being introduced, while art in many Primary Schools suffers from a critical shortage of materials.

In 1977 the Gallery published extracts from the Schools Exhibition adjudicators' reports by Arthur Azevedo and Babette Fitzgerald. The judges stressed the importance of 'found' materials in children's art and the need to improvise. To depend on expensive imported materials is to inhibit the child. Since then, a refreshing variety has crept into Schools work including a very wide range of types of collage and 3D work. Sometimes, rumour has it, creativity has overcome moral discretion: Self: 'Let's have a wire toys competition for the Midlands.' Public official: 'If you do, I can say ''Goodbye'' to all my wire security fences!'

Current developments in the arts have included the restructuring of the system of Arts Councils into a state supported network of bodies concerned with co-ordinating arts activities in the interest of the people as a whole. Regional Cultural Officers have been appointed, and a large number of community cultural festivals have been held. A network of local Culture Centres fostering the community arts in the local rural centres is to be set up, so that the arts are restored to the people.

With independence the National Gallery, which had latterly been responsible to the Ministry of Justice, was transferred to the new Ministry of Education and Culture. This enabled it to become more involved with the lives of the people. A new educational policy for the Gallery has emerged, essentially with two dimensions focussed on Mrs Doreen Sibanda and Mr Paul Wade respectively. Mrs Sibanda, by accepting dance entries at the 1983 Schools Exhibition, seemed to be moving towards a holistic interpretation of the arts. Dance and drama items had been held in conjunction with exhibition at the Gallery before, but with the exception of dance performances during I.C.A.C. were not presented as part of an overall artistic event.

Mrs Sibanda's work includes practical art classes for school-children held at the Gallery; help and advice to schools; small suitcase exhibitions of sculptures and photographs of paintings for schools; and handouts on artists and their techniques. Put together in Travelling Boxes, these little exhibitions tour schools, spending one term at a time in a region. There are also self-guided tours for children to the Gallery with handouts and quiz booklets, and volunteer-guided tours. Other planned activities include among others in-service courses for teachers, a slide loan scheme, and a mobile touring unit to take exhibitions to the rural areas.

Mr Wade built up the B.A.T. Workshop and required neither fees nor entry qualifications except for a reasonable degree of skill in drawing. It runs a two-year course with a full-time attendance of 15 students in the first year. Landscape and portrait painting, abstract and figure sculpture in clay, wood, serpentine, card and plaster, lino-cutting and woodblock print-ing, silkscreen and etching, textile printing, tapestry weaving, batik and tie and dye, and drawing for expression are taught with specialization in one of Painting, Textiles, Printmaking and Sculpture in the Second Year. It is hoped to teach scrapmetal-welding as well. Eventually it is hoped to have a three-year certificate course with specialist tutors in all key areas.

The position by 1985 is therefore reasonably sound. There is a vast amount of stone-carving, mainly for the tourist trade, with a small number of international artists like National Gal-lery's Thomas Mukarobgwa and like Nicholas Mukombera-nwa, trained by Fr Groeber, John Takawira who worked with the Burdett-Couttses and Henry Muzengere, encouraged by Tom Blomefield. These artists concentrate on themes from folklore and traditional beliefs, though Thomas Mukarobgwa, for example, is a convinced Christian. There is some work of a fairly high quality in representational carving of animals, for example by a Paterson artist, Chiadzwa.

There is woodcarving of a rather variable quality; top quality wood is not available and little effective use is made of the grain but some pleasant work has been done, mainly for religious pur-poses. Craft-work generally has been encouraged with some success, notably in traditional pottery-work, by such artists as Mrs Esther Nhliziyo and Violet Tagariro.

Painting, despite the early successes of Paterson's pupils and of such artists as the well-known John Hlatywayo remains of a low level because of the high cost of materials and a national shortage of art teachers. However, batik and costume pattern design are developing fairly quickly.

On the whole the artistic potential of the country remains very high but inhibited by financial constraints. The future should be extremely interesting to observe.

As for the intangible benefits of the work of Paterson and the other art teachers, three areas come to mind. They encouraged the imaginative and personal development of their students. They fostered through the artists' communities their social and spiritual development. They helped to give the students a sense of self-respect and respect for their country and led to increased respect for them, and Zimbabwe abroad.

The artistic achievements of a people help overcome pre-judice against them. The arts are international and assert, across national and community boundaries, the unity of the human race. By fostering the arts, by showing that the disabled, the outcast and abandoned were capable of great achievements, Paterson and his colleagues asserted the spiritual, unifying forces of love and compassion against the materialistic, divisive forces of selfishness and greed. Love, like art, has no boundaries of colour, class or creed except those man's selfishness chooses to raise against it. Paterson in particular asserted the value of manual workers in an Africa which tends to despise them; of physical and mentally disabled people; of black people in a world ruled then by whites; of children in a world dominated by adults; and of women in a male dominated society. By drawing

his artists from all over Central Africa, he denied nationalism. By refusing to lay down competitive entry standards, he asserted the value of interest and enthusiasm against the prevalent passion for collecting diplomas as passports to more pay. In short, Paterson set up a Christian standard in love and integrity which he expressed through art teaching and which is still extremely relevant to Africa today.

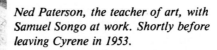

Ned Paterson, the teacher of art, with Samuel Songo at work. Shortly before leaving Cyrene in 1953.

1.   *The Plinth: Start of the Journey*

SCOTLAND: ABERDEEN: 1895 – 1901

Edward Paterson was born on Jan 2nd 1895 in Aberdeen, Scotland. His father James worked there as a grocer's assistant in Lumsden and Gibson's shop at 95 Union Street. The family had a background of adventurous poverty.

Ned's mother, Elsie Mary Dougal, was a fiery little woman from Hull and the windswept Orkneys. Her father, Captain Dougal, had been the captain of a Hull-based tea-clipper. He had artistic tastes and brought back pieces of Chinese pottery which Ned would inherit. When his ship went down off the Paternosters in the Java Seas he was the only casualty. He left a widow and seven children who had a hard struggle to make ends meet, and a fierce pride in the hard work which kept them from destitution.

Ned's father had also learned to overcome poverty by work. James's father was an illiterate and good natured farm-worker at Cruden who had two illegitimate children and then married James's mother. From her James learned to read, but up to the age of 18 he had no other formal education. From 8 to 17 James worked on various farms. When he was 13 he was paid his whole year's wages in advance in a £5 note which his illiterate father used as a spill to light his tobacco pipe. The family never recovered the money, so the lad had to do a year's work for no pay.

At 18 James was asked what he would like most and answered 'six months at school'. His six months over, he did seven years apprenticeship at the shop in Aberdeen. Then he married Elsie Dougal, and had six children, one dying in in-fancy. Jim was the eldest, then Ned, born in 1895, the year of the 830 km London to Aberdeen railways races, Douglas, Gordon and his twin sister who died, and Leslie, born abroad, followed.

Though Ned left Aberdeen when he was very young, he was very proud of his birthplace, the glittering granite city with its singing church-bells, shimmering spires and towering factory chimneys, and its varied smells. The shop was a child's delight with its monumental cairns of unwrapped goods: mountainous 30kg cheeses, huge tins of syrup, sides of smoky smelling bacon hanging from great hooks up in the ceiling, chests of tea from the Far East and sugar from the West Indies, crates of fruit and vegetables, magnificently coloured, and the pleasure of soft women's voices across the counter.

Aberdeen was a proud city with a thousand years of history. She was a trading centre with new railway lines to London and to Wick. Her ships sailed the world's seas. She had been the home of Thomson's White Star Line, whose towering white-sailed clippers, such as the famous *Thermopylae*, danced the seas to Australia and the East.

She was a town where many peoples mixed freely together, where Celt and Lowlander, laird and labourer, lived and worked more or less side by side. This encouraged a sense of freedom and a readiness to work for the rights of others, without regard to race or creed. The town's patron saint is St Nicholas, Santa Claus, the patron saint of children. The set of bells on St Nicholas Church were, and still are, the biggest in all Britain and rang out over land and sea to fisher, farmer, sailor, shopkeeper, dockworker and dominie the welcome message of

Good Will. In time of fog or expected storm they could summon home the fishing fleet. At Christmas and at Hogmanay they sounded across the expectant city the singing changes of the passing years.

James loved music and showed it in his choice of faith. In a poor land, the Presbyterian Kirk was dour and stark. Art and much music were distrusted and despised as sinful luxuries. But James raised his family in the less austere Episcopalian (Anglican) ways, fortunately for Ned's future talents.

Aberdeen is a good place for future artists to live. She is, and was, a lovely city. Her granite and sandstone buildings, pink and pale green and silver-grey and gold, shine sometimes with a shimmering gem-like crystal beauty. Her gently drifting cloud-patterned skies look down on green fields, hills, soft sands and wrinkling ever-changing blue-grey seas. The silver city on the golden sands has her own music in the songs of birds, ship's sirens, distant cries of wandering gulls, the soft winds' moan and the stray bark of seals. She was a good home for a future soldier and amateur archaeologist, too. Buchan and the hills around have been settled and fought over for thousands of years. A single hillock may contain a thousand pre-historic graves. Buchan families were close, bound in a fierce pride of loving and quarrelling, working and wooing. "Bitin' and scrattin's the Scotch wye o'wooin'" and "if there's a hair t' clash aboot, they'll mak a tetcher o't" were local proverbs of those days.

The fierce bond of kinship could crush the individual or release great fires of creativity and love. Even the Aberdeen emblem and motto, three silver castles on a blood-red ground with the motto 'Bon Accord', — stress the strength in unity which the Patersons would show in Africa.

This was a time of great excitement for the young lad. The Anglo-Boer wars were on. In 1900 Britain went wild over the relief of Mafeking, held by Baden-Powell, founder of the Boy Scouts, against a Boer seige. Had Mafeking fallen, it was said, Botswana and even Zimbabwe would have fallen under Boer rule. Mafeking was seen as the turning of the tide of war after the defeats of Magersfontein, Stormberg and Colenso. Ned was enthralled by the Mafeking parade down Aberdeen's main street, Union Street. Units of a Highland regiment marched proudly down the street, their colourful kilts swinging as they walked, accompanied by the triumphant skirling of bagpipe music and the rhythmic beat of the drums.

The glamour, the excitement and the idealism of that time, when Britain seemed a protector of the weak against the bullying Boers, would never wholly leave Ned, while he saw the setbacks of life as a succession of Makekings which he was confident could with courage be relieved. Whatever hardships life held, he was sure that hard work would bring a successful outcome.

SOUTH AFRICA: NOUPOORT: 1901 – 09

In 1901 James Paterson took his family to South Africa's Karoo wilderness to escape suspected T.B. James went first, to get a job and accommodation, and was taken on by Elsworth's, a grocer's shop in Noupoort.

Noupoort, 'Narrow Gate' (Matt 7:13), was a small Karoo town used as a base by General French's British army. The population was swollen to 23 000 by troops.

Elsie and the children sailed out by Cape Town to Port Elizabeth, and went on to Noupoort by train. The last few kms were travelled at high speed on the footplate of the engine, for General Jan Smuts's forces had broken through the British lines and the heavy coaches were too slow. Ned was thrilled, but Elsie, bouncing on the tender, complained 'Why's it called a tender when I'm the one that's tender?'

The children settled in happily, though when they first saw the house with its mud floor and corrugated iron roof they thought it was a stable. The security arrangements interested them: there was barbed wire all round the town hung with little tins which jangled to warn the sentries if anyone tried to cross it. Secure behind the fence the children could enjoy the glamour of army parades, especially the colour and music of funerals.

When it was a Scottish regiment, they would follow the soldiers with the coffins and listen to the bagpipes playing 'The Flowers of the Forest', the Flodden lament. On the way back from the cemetery the bands played cheery tunes such as 'The Barren Rocks of Aden' ('The Green Hills of Tyrol'). This link of death with cheerful music and colourful togetherness in childhood would help Ned later on. In later life his cheerful acceptance of death as 'just another adventure' would help him tremendously to care for the sick, the dying and the bereaved, and even bring a touch of gaiety into his own funeral. For in the best Scottish sense, he learned to see death as at worst a release from suffering, but more often, like a journey to Tir nan Og, the Celtic Islands of the Blessed, it was a joyful beginning.

Noupoort was a railways centre where three lines met and the Cape Railways had workshops.

After the war the railway system gradually crept north, opening up new frontiers for trade and industry, and all sorts of people passed through the town. In addition there were many people like James Paterson, refugees from illness to the dry Karoo. As the Paterson children grew older they could take advantage of dramatic societies, music groups, and well-stocked libraries. They were encouraged by their parents to read widely and well. There were no comic books, no films, 'no thrillers beyond Dickens' and of course no T.V. Instead, they entertained themselves, sketching, writing, making their own music, looking around them, listening, whittling toys, and so on. The drawing seems to have started with Ned's father, who drew cats to amuse the children. Even the contrast between Aberdeen and Noupoort may have sharply heightened Ned's intensity of observation, while another important figure was Robert Bunting-Smith, M.A. from Paisley. Bunting-Smith was dying of T.B., says Ned. He filled in the time as he died by teaching literacy, numeracy, and singing by the sol-fa method. He called his school 'Naauwpoort Public School' and he encouraged Ned to draw. In addition, his deep religious faith, complete lack of self-pity, and total involvement with his school children would be a great influence. He firmly believed that even a child cannot escape responsibility to others. Ned and his brothers Jim and Douglas showed this responsibility early in a striking, though curious, way.

Ned's father James had learned to play the little pedal organ in the Anglican Church. One Sunday in 1904 Ned ran away from Church where he was supposed to pump the organ for his father. He joined his brothers Jim and Douglas and they wandered along the railway. They found some trucks had rolled backwards and fallen across the line. Knowing a train was due, Ned ran to warn the Station Master to change the signals while Jim and Douglas watched the tracks. The Cape Railways gave Ned an engraved silver pocket watch for his public spiritedness. James's comments are not recorded.

Attendance at Church might be voluntary, but attendance at school certainly was not. James valued his sons' education very highly. In 1962 Ned wrote 'I had to walk two miles to school. Having got the father I had, I got away in good time and I got a prize. Never absent, never late for seven years. Often Noupoort was bitterly cold. On one day of snow, many sheep died. Only seven of us out of 200–300 arrived at school. What a marvel my dad was!'

His mother Elsie was also strong-willed. Mrs Hugh Finn writes 'His mother was a tiny virago. Once the boys could not stand her tirade any longer and picked her up and parked her on

Ned with aunt Polly (Aberdeen)

The Paterson family: James Paterson sen. with James the eldest son; mother Elsie holding one of the twins (Gordon & sister who died). Douglas on right and Edward (Ned) seated in front. The maid is holding the other twin. Leslie followed later.
(Photo taken at Noupoort)

Ned the scout having done service in Namibia (1915)

Ned (right) with his elder brother James; they were called up during World War I with the Transvaal Scottish Regiment.

top of the wardrobe. There she was left to fume impotently until someone remembered to collect her.' Elsie once said of Ned 'What have I done that God has given me a mad son?'

On pleasanter days the boys used to go for long walks in the Karoo. Ned loved its colours, its soft golds and mauves and reds, its greyish soil, its yellowed pebbles, its grasses, its mosses and lichens and its insect life. He loved the miracles of beauty and life in the wilderness, in a land sometimes so dry that it seemed amazing that anything at all could grow, yet which burst into an explosion of fertility when storms came.

'Consider the lilies of the field, how they grow' (Matt. 6:28). Life in the Karoo, and later Kalahari and Namib deserts, amazed Ned even more. A darting sand-lizard or koggelmander, perfectly adapted for its arid life, astonished and excited him. The wilderness taught him above all that though a miracle of nature, man is very little more than a handful of dust, utterly dependent on love to survive. Yet this handful of dust, this speck on a vast landscape, can create works of great beauty. And the sun creeping over the Karoo, changing the colours and shapes of rocks and hills, grasslands and dwellings, taught him about painting, relief carving, and sculpture. From the sun and the dry land he learned how to make still shapes seem alive.

BENONI: 1909 – 14

In 1909, when Ned had completed his primary schooling, James realized there was not to be work for his sons in the town. There were now five of them, for Leslie had been born at Noupoort, and five sons were too many to feed.

The Patersons moved 600 km north of Benoni, a new mining town on the Ridge of White Waters, the Witwatersrand, 30 km from Johannesburg. Founded in 1904, Benoni, Son of Sorrow (Gen. 35:16 – 18) is named after Joseph's brother Benjamin, the Son of the South.

Benoni was a rough mining town. There were billiard saloons, shooting galleries, a roller-skating rink, a theatre, and occasional dances where the men hurled their partners about vigorously. Travelling shows were frequent. Film shows started in 1909 and were a great success. By 1912 there were three cinemas showing silent films. The great craze of 1909 – 10 was roller-skating at the rink. There were wheelbarrow races, chariot races, hockey and football matches, and fancy dress carnivals — all on roller skates. In addition, illegal gambling dens flourished.

Five years earlier a large force of mine workers had started to arrive from the north of China. These Chinese coolies were hard workers, but at times some of them broke out of the mine compounds and ran wild. Hence an *East Rand Express* (Aug 19, 1904) headline: 'A Reign of Disorder. Burglaries, Assaults and Outrages. Marauding Chinese Fired On.'

James built a house for his family at 97 Elstone Avenue. He got a job with the grocers Lindsay and Pirie, later working with the grocers Gray, Smith and Co. Jim got a job with a mining company and took up a career as a reduction worker with various gold mines.

Ned's younger brothers Douglas, Gordon and Leslie were sent to the local school. Douglas and Gordon later went into banking, and Douglas became Barclays Benoni Branch Bank Manager. Leslie later became an overseer fitter and turner. They all remained in Benoni.

James and Elsie remained in the house in Elstone Avenue all their lives. James died at the ripe age of 92 about 1950, and Elsie died in 1957. The family sold the house to a church as a clergyman's home about 1980.

In 1909 young Ned became an office boy in the Magistrate's Office. The first law case he was asked to report on concerned sexual relations with animals. He says he was so fascinated, 'ears flapping', that he nearly forgot to take notes.

In the evenings he was sent to the local night school, at first as a pupil. However, Bunting-Smith had taught him so much that, still only 14, he was made the teacher in charge of the second year, Std II. It was a very rough area of town. His mother was terrified of it, but Ned greatly enjoyed observing the turbulent lives of the Chinese, African and European mine workers. He loved their rough vitality and explosive energy, but was saddened by their impetuous violence and especially the endless drunken knifings when they gambled.

Ned was vigorous himself. He played a lot of hockey. He was a boxer and taught boxing to local blacks. And at some point he acquired a girl-friend, Miss 'Tickey' (Threepence) Asplin.

Ned did not stay long as the Magistrate, Richard Colson, shocked at his employment in such surroundings, had him transferred to a mine office, and he was later employed by Benoni Municipality, earning over £32 a year by 1914. He had also become a part-time soldier.

In 1912, aged 17, Ned joined the Transvaal Scottish Regiment on a 'territorial' basis. During the week he worked at his office job and at the weekends he went to Johannesburg to learn how to fight and to parade in a cheerfully coloured Murray of Atholl kilt. War with Germany was drawing close, and German forces were near. She ruled Namibia and Tanzania, and wanted to expand in Africa.

WORLD WAR I

War broke out in August 1914. At once the Transvaal Scottish were called up. To Ned's intense annoyance they were sent to fight in Namibia in kilts without underwear — hot, very conspicuous, and extremely vulnerable to dust and sharp-biting sandflies. The penalty for wearing underwear Ned claims was anointing with golden syrup and condensed milk to attract more sandflies. They marched, he says, for 342 days without firing a single shot in anger.

The beauty and the vastness of that desolate majestic land, however, greatly appealed to Ned. They helped him to build on his childhood experiences in the Karoo. And his Karoo excitement at fertility in the desert was further awakened when not a man's wells but the impersonal winds brought nourishing water. 'I was in the Namib Desert for a year. Heavenly! The oldest desert in the world,' he later wrote to Lady Le Gros Clark. 'In winter the west winds fill the desert with a million seeds. The summer winds bring rain and a rush of vegetation, with all sorts of life, but no fear. One can measure with one's eye the light years separating the stars and know we are nothing' (10 Dec. 1968). But the desert affected other people differently. Many years later in Namibia an Afrikaans magistrate would bitterly ask Ned why so few Germans had been killed! Ned glorified in the vast solitudes of the wilderness, domed with the night sky. Others just found loneliness and empty silence, and a lack of things to do.

In 1915 Ned returned to South Africa, and went, first with the 9th South African Infantry and later in 1917 as an officer and instructor with the Kings African Rifles (black troops), to East Africa. The East African campaign fought in tropical forest against the forces of the amazing German General von Lettow-Vorbeck, was a grim but valuable experience, for several reasons. Von Lettow-Vorbeck's forces, black and white, lightly armed and swiftly moving, held down a vastly superior but brutally disciplined British and South African army by courage, intelligence, imagination and inspired leadership.

Paterson described this time as 'the dullest and most unpleasant experience I had during the war.' He disliked camping in the forest, 'scared times out of number' by the 'creepy-crawlies' 'things with green squidgy bodies, vermilion warts and yellow hair dragging their loathly selves towards my bed, things that just don't go bump in the night'. These were the ever-watching, unnameable, seemingly malevolent 'fear in the trees', and guerillas might also attack at night.

Ned was shocked at the treatment given black troops. 'For a trifling offence, such as a button off his uniform, the black ''culprit'' was given a couple of full-arm smacks in the face'. Once, for buttoning up a loose button he was reported to his captain who said, 'We are trying to make them soldiers, *Sir*, not milksops'.

'For a more serious breach of discipline the offender was laid face downwards and naked. Then a wet cloth was placed over his back and buttocks and cuts administered by a sergeant using a five-foot sjambok made of hippopotamus hide-long, black and tapering into flexibility — dreadful weapon called ''kibobo''.'

I was near vomiting when such dreadful punishment took place on parade — the ''maibobo'' of the sufferer, the spurts of blood, the crimsoning cloth.

In May 1918, after ten unhappy months, Paterson was sent back to South Africa with fever and jaundice. He was glad to get 'home'.

BRAKPAN: 1919 – 20

After the War Ned became the first (Acting) Town Clerk of Brakpan, Salty Pool, which split off from Benoni 6 km away in 1919. He found the Council bitterly divided and faction ridden, not to mention corrupt. He claims some abused their power to get municipal gravel for their own paths. Disgusted, Ned

8

resigned. In later years Ned would work extremely hard to keep his family and community loving, forgiving and united.

What now? Ned wanted to get away from the Rand and to develop his talents. He was also in search of a personal philosophy.

Bunting-Smith had encouraged him to draw, and during the War his humorous sketches of his fellow-officers had won him many friends. He decided to go to London to study art.

He was awarded an army grant of £160 a year for three years to study at London's Central School of Arts and Crafts. Later he would joke that his 'Naauwpoort Public School' background let the authorities think he was from a famous Public School, like Eton or Harrow. He was certainly as proud of his school as many Etonians of theirs.

Ned during his training in England (1923)

2. Training

Paterson was 25. His life had been rough. He was a 'damn tough', a 'cowboy type', a 'man's man', potentially a resounding misfit in the delicate atmosphere of an art school. But he was not alone. The universities and colleges were full of demobilised soldiers, trying to adapt from the hell of the trenches and find meaning in civilian life. The Brookes, Owens, Sorleys and Thomases had been killed. Britain alone had lost nearly a million dead. The world had lost some ten million. In addition, about twenty million people had died in the 1918 influenza epidemic.

Ned was less disillusioned than the others. He had never served in the trenches. His poverty and the rough realism of his youth had cushioned him against the shocks of war. He had lost some friends in East Africa but was more shocked by cruel discipline and urban corruption than by lunacies of warfare. He was certainly agnostic, but his basic faith in human nature was untouched.

His grandfather had brought back Chinese ware from the Paternosters. Ned's Benoni night school had been in a partly Chinese slum district. Now it was to Chinese art that he turned for inspiration. He found in the vitality, the energy, the intricacy and the spiritual profundity of Chinese art a source of tremendous excitement. He wandered the back streets of Soho seeking 'objects which cried out to be possessed and loved,' such as an ivory nude used by doctors and war horse snorting in the breeze, excited by battle. He loved the Chinese section of the British Museum, and there he met and got to know the Keeper of Oriental Prints and Drawings, the poet Laurence Binyon.

BINYON

Laurence Binyon (1869−1943) was a clergyman's son. In the 1880s he was a student at Trinity College Oxford when Charles Gore was a Fellow there. In 1892 Gore founded the Community of the Resurrection which had already had a branch house in Johannesburg in 1903. A fellow student and friend of Binyon's was Arthur S. Cripps, a disciple of Gore, later known as a saintly missionary and campaigner for black rights in Zimbabwe. Binyon and Cripps produced a volume of poems called *Primavera* together in Oxford in 1890.

Ned's friendship with Binyon started one day when Binyon accidentally dropped his wallet. Ned picked it up, recognized Binyon, and got into conversation. He then arranged for Binyon to give a lecture on Chinese art at the Central.

The opening of Binyon's lecture had a striking, perhaps accidental, resemblance to the Ceremony of Light which opens Toc. H. meetings. 'Binyon plunged the room into darkness. He asked the students to imagine they were in a tomb. The only light was on the rostrum, which enabled us to see the white knuckles of his hands clenching the reading desk as he spoke, twisting his love of Chinese art as a woman wrings out a garment.

9

I for one was glad of the darkness it hid the feeling he gave me and which I still have' (7.6.72). Then, amid the darkness, there was another soft light. Binyon switched on a slide, showing strange and beautiful objects, concealed in the tomb's darkness, perhaps for thousands of years, awaiting discovery by strangers, revealing their artists' messages to them.

In his letter to Lady Le Gros Clark just quoted, Ned compares this experience to awakening after death to rebirth into fellowship with God.

At the time, however, Ned was still an agnostic. Binyon seems however to have deepened his ability to respond to both art and poetry, and possibly to other people as well, by thinking of the distances in time and culture between an artist and his eventual audience.

In Chinese art, Ned came particularly to love T'ang art (618–916 A.D.). In this art landscapes are common. Man appears puny, dwarved by nature's vastness. There are flowing lines, fluid forms, minutely observed details, and bold colours. There is stress on the dynamic qualities of power held in check and energy on the verge of exploding into action.

Binyon's poetry also unquestionably influenced Ned. Binyon's answer to the bitterness, pessimism and disillusionment which produced the Roaring Twenties was a transcendent vision. The significance of our lives, as of our art, is not completed when we die, provided we live energetically, honestly, and for other people or a cause. Just as the work of art is not dead because it is concealed in a tomb, for someone may find it, so what we live for is more important than what we are. 'Because the time has strip us bare. Of all things but the thing we are. . . . Rejoice! we die, the cause is never dead,' Binyon says in *To the End. In Before Dawn* he even asserts for the soldiers 'we ourselves are Fate'. But most striking is the most famous line he wrote, in *For the Fallen*. 'They shall grow not old,' which is inscribed on many war memorials. Paterson firm-

ly asserted that Binyon meant there to be a pause after 'grow'. The idea is that with death, with the end of earthly life, the growing is not over. Those who from dedication have accepted death, or who live life to the full in loving service, will continue to grow after it 'into the likeness of Christ,' and have been called to further service beyond the grave.

A philosophy of this kind, however attractive, requires a more solid expression to become convincing. Paterson continued in search of himself and his goal in life, and continued to study at the Central.

THE CENTRAL

The Central School of Arts and Crafts was to inspire Ned in a different way from Binyon, and without his realizing it. It would help to channel the molten lava of his explosive spirit and to civilize the inner revolutionary. In addition, as an expression of William Morris's idea of a community of artists and craftsmen, the Central would affect Ned's view of what a school of art should be throughout his life. We find his idea reflected in both Ned's Cyrene projects, in his vision of potential roles of the second Cyrene as a Culture Centre for Zimbabwe (ideally as one of a large number of such centres), and even later in his hopes for the Nyarutsetso and Farayi Art Centres in Harare. We find it partly reflected in the Workshop School of the National Gallery, on the Board of which Paterson served. We find it further reflected in Ned's personal desire to be versatile in different arts and crafts. And we find it in his preoccupations on the one hand with self-help and on the other with the spiritual need people have for an attractive living environment preferably decorated by themselves. This living environment, moreover, extends outside the home to bring nature's beauty into the thoroughfare and the market-place. Ned like Morris learned to see the hostility of man's spirit to the imposed ugliness of industrialism, and to assert not only that artistic ability is generally distributed but also in effect that access to beauty, and to insights through beauty, are universal rights and needs.

The Central School had been founded in 1896. A product of the Arts and Crafts Movement, it played an important role in the development of Art Education in Britain and to a lesser extent in Europe and Africa. The spirit behind the Arts and Crafts Movement was John Ruskin (1819–1900), the writer, art critic and social reformer. Ruskin revered beauty in nature for its own sake, felt art had a high moral function, and was passionately opposed both to industrialism and to the use of art teaching merely to improve industrial design. Ruskin's vehement hostility to industrialisation is still relevant today. 'You must either make a tool of the creature or a man of him,' he wrote. He proclaimed that true art is a process of joyful growth. 'All work is done in the spirit of the artist, aims at the perfection of the artist, and announces the joy of the artist.' This philosophy would make a life-long contribution to Ned's work in art and education. It would be combined with Morris's view that all men's right to 'eager life while we live, is above all things the aim of art.'

William Morris (1834–96) was inspired by Ruskin's ideals and vision, which he found 'a revelation'. Influenced by Ruskin and the priest-novelist-historian Charles Kingsley (1818–75), Morris built an ideal of artistic socialism, of art as a necessary liberator of the spirit of everyone. He boldly claimed that 'in a reasonable life the perception and creation of beauty are as necessary to man as his daily bread.'

In reaction to the Victorian art training in schools, which tended to consist of copying formal geometric figures, Ruskin wanted to use art to train the perception and observation of nature.

He saw moral uplift in the accurate reproduction of the forms and beauties of nature. Morris went beyond this, accepting the need for the imagination to select and develop forms and harmonies based on those in nature.

On Ruskin's human ideals Morris built a vision of society itself as a network of intimate, caring, creative communities or workshops. In these communities people would work together in harmony for the common good.

The arts would be interdependent. Architecture would provide an appropriately harmonious environment. Creative craftsmen — painters, smiths, decorators, weavers, textile glassware and furniture makers would come together, work together and stimulate each other. The first of these workshop communities was launched in 1861. He himself combined artistic, administrative and poetic gifts. From the 1890s he had a decisive influence on art education. In 1896 W.R. Lethaby (1857–1931), an architect friend, became first Principal of the new Central School of Arts and Crafts, and the Board of Education approved a new Alternative, more imaginative syllabus in Art for Schools. In 1897 the Royal College of Art was founded. In 1898, Morris's friend Walter Crane, the illustrator and designer of prints became its Principal. Crane had already been Director at Manchester (1893) and Art Director at Reading University College (1896). Lethaby, who remained Principal at the Central School till his death, was Professor of Design at the Royal College of Art from 1900 to 1918.

The Arts and Crafts Movement had considerable impact in Europe, especially in Germany, where it influenced the reaction to materialism and the cult of machinery — Walther Gropius, founder of the Weimar Bauhaus in 1919, declared: 'The artist has power to endow the lifeless machine-made object with a soul.'

In England the Movement influenced examinations. In 1913, for example, life-drawing was included in the London

Higher School Certificate examination, and in 1918 a national network of examinations in art was introduced.

One important member of the Arts and Crafts movement was a Catholic, Eric Gill, designer, engraver and sculptor, best remembered now as a father of modern type design. Gill's Stations of the Cross in Westminster Catholic Cathedral profoundly moved Ned in his London years. Gill's style, with its flowing lines and simplified features, may have influenced Ned's artistic output especially in bas-relief and indirectly affected the work of his pupils and Cyrene students. Gill also ran an artists' community, combining craftsmanship and agriculture. 'Arts and crafts,' he wrote, 'are means to the service of God and our fellows. I hope I have done something towards reintegrating bed and board, the small farm and the workshop, the home and the school, earth and heaven.' One of his boldest statements, on the religiosity of all art, is this: 'Man collaborates with God in creating — that is what he is for. . . . Man is that part of creation which can praise his Creator. He is in misery unless he obeys this call.' Gill's friend Donald Attwater combined careers as a writer of books on the Catholic saints and as a skilled craftsman in glass.

Of Ned's days at the Central, Morris Kestelman writes, 'It was a very strange and exhilarating new world, full of ex-service men, tough and boisterous.' After copying casts of Roman, Greek, Medieval and Renaissance figures, the students were allowed to copy from life. Men and women worked in separate classes, the Principal arranging an individual timetable for each student. The Paterson generation worked 'with great verve' and enthusiasm and generated a very bohemian atmosphere, very warm and intimate.' The main areas of study were furniture, book-binding, fine printing, book-illustration, silversmithing, pottery, textile design, etching, lithography and wood-engraving under Noel Rooke. The quality of drawing, Kestelman remembers, was outstanding, second only to the

Slade. Teachers included F. Jackson A.R.A., the illustrator A.S. Hartrick, James Grant the etcher, Bernard Meninsky, and the Vorticist artist William Roberts. In 1890 Roberts had associated with Wyndham Lewis, Henri Gaudier-Brzcska and Epstein in the Cubist Vorticist school, which broke up in 1916. Led by the shock of the War away from Abstract art, Roberts simplified human figures into forces of lines and planes which have grim dynamism. James Fitton (R.A. 1954) was a fellow student with Paterson, whom Kestelman remembers as 'a Wild West character'. This suggests Ned softened considerably after coming to the School. Ned remembered how he was affectionately addressed when he first came. 'You damn colonial! You have only been here five minutes and you think you own the place!'

Ned's own reaction to the School was decidedly negative. 'My first lesson in the life class was a terrifying experience with a hairy woman, nude, little curly hairs all down her thighs. When I told my Aberdeen aunt she was upset and said she would write to my mother.' Unfortunately Ned, sharing Ruskin's view of art as perception, had a heightened awareness of the inner vitality of ugliness as well as beauty; hence his success as a caricaturist. He found it too easy to laugh at ugliness. One incident turned him against art for art's sake. He was sketching a fishing boat. The owner came up, furious and contemptuous. 'That's no ma boat. That boat could never sail on land or sea.' Ned accepted the ridicule.

One story helps explain Ned's reputation at the Central. At the Cyrene London show in 1949 Ned met W. Robins, one of his teachers at the Central, by then President of the Royal Society of Painter Etchers. 'I went up and said, "You don't remember me?" He said, "Yes! Paterson, and you were a wicked little b---! Do you remember putting the bottle of nitric acid near the ammonia bottle to see the explosion?" ' Ned coyly remarks, 'I rather think that was true.'

THE CALEDONIAN

His spontaneous humour attracted Ned to the Caledonian Market, where he recovered a faith in human goodness and tenacity which he felt he had lost.

The Caledonian Market took place in the London Borough of Islington. Islington had once been a country village, and for centuries supplied London's milk. The biggest Cattle Market in Europe arose there, providing fresh meat until canned and frozen meat reduced demand.

The 3½ ha site became the most famous street market in London. Before the Second World War nearly 2 000 pedlars and anything up to 100 000 potential customers at once thronged the twice-weekly market. It was a great place for bargain hunting, bright colours, and cheery cockney humour.

The Market, transferred to Bermondsey after the Second World War, was one of the sights of London.

The tremendous energy and cheery comedy of the Market appealed to Ned. His faith in basic human values had been damaged alike by the cruel futility of the War and the envious corruption of peace. An Ethical Society in Clapham had seemed to him merely to spout 'Words, words, words'.

But the Market restored his faith in the goodness and endurance of man, without which faith in a God is perhaps impossible. Ned's enthusiasm was so great that he was commissioned to design posters advertising the Market for London Transport Tramways. He also did a poster for the 1922 Devonshire House Fete.

Two exhibitions shown in London during his time at the Central may well have influenced Ned's later use of art. In 1921 an exhibition of work by Franz Cizek's young Viennese children toured Britain and was a tremendous success. In 1923 Marion Richardson, later a very influential London School In-

spector, held an exhibition of work by her Dudley Girls' High School pupils at the Independent Gallery in London.

Cizek encouraged his children to express their feelings in art. He looked for innocence, simplicity and self-expression. Art had to be fun for them or it was valueless. The teacher should guide and encourage, but never formally instruct. He should 'let the children teach themselves.'

Marion Richardson's High School girls produced remarkable pictures of the world around them expressing their feelings. In her 1923 exhibition catalogue she explained that she encouraged her girls to 'concentrate upon and give expression to mental images founded upon their own observations. . . . Often the children succeed in inventing their own subject'. One of Ned's Cyrene pupils explained his own method more simply: 'First I think and then I draw my think.'

The period at the Central, then, contributed to Ned's understanding of art and life. It also trained him as a craftsman in wood bas-reliefs. It gave him figurative and decorative craft skills. It developed a passionate interest in antiquities as revelations of the social experience of the past, and it awakened his sensitivity to other cultures and to people and artifacts as the expressions of cultural experience.

PAGET

By 1923, Ned was in search of a job. Noel Rooke, the Chief Examiner at the Central, looked at one of his drawings and commented of Ned's future career 'it's something fairly big — but it isn't Art'. Ned was perhaps too impatient, too honest with himself, and too practical to be an artist. He was offered a job as Drawing Master at Rugby School but, afraid of the boys, turned it down. He also turned down a job at the Central School, feeling uninspired by it.

He claims to have been converted to Christianity by the obvious absurdity of the Bible. A work so irrational, so ridiculous, could only have its influence, he felt, if it were true. In any event he felt he belonged in Africa and not in London, so he returned home.

The vicar in Benoni was Edward Paget, a fiery advocate of the poor. Paget (1886 – 1971) was son of the Bishop of Oxford and had been influenced by Gore. After a time working in the London slums he had come to Benoni in 1914 and started youth work. He was a great success with teenagers in Benoni and was a conspicuous figure riding round the mines on his Douglas motor cycle. Like Ned he served in the East Africa campaign, receiving the M.C., yet he was an outspoken critic of incompetent administration. In the 1920 influenza epidemic he organized volunteer auxiliary medical teams in the hospitals and in the slums of Benoni, and ran welfare services for the miners' families during the 1922 Rand Riots. Paget believed strongly in practical Christianity and divided his parish into twenty districts, each with its own unpaid lay leadership team. He set a personal example, accessible to people day and night. He was a sportsman, disapproving of excessive formality in church services, and his impact on Paterson was direct and dynamic: 'through him I became a priest.' 'He got me ordained.'

Fr Edward Francis Paget was elected Bishop of Mashonaland in 1925. In 1955 he became the first Archbishop of the new Province of Central Africa. He retired in 1957 and died in 1971.

3. Vocation

RAILWAY MISSIONER: 1924

Ned's first job in his new career in South Africa was as a Railway Missioner, travelling the railway lines, teaching whatever skills and knowledge he had, over a thousand mile circuit. Most of the people he met were Afrikaans speakers, and Ned's Karoo childhood helped. Ned spoke slangy popular Afrikaans easily. His army days helped, too. He knew plenty of Afrikaans slang, which could spice his stories. He later got a startling reputation for using unconventional language in sermons, not for effect but because it was the language of the slums.

The Railway Missioner usually travelled in a caboose — van on a goods train. There he made his home. A bed, table, chair, bookcase and a little cooker provided his needs. The train wandered from station to station, from siding to siding. At the longer stops the missioner got out, met people, and if there was time might hold a service or prayer meeting.

However, Ned disliked being carted around and realized that the train passed by many communities. He wanted to meet everyone. So he bought a sturdy bicycle. With his pack on his back he pedalled many weary kilometres on dusty roads from station to station under the beating sun. He slept where he could, in huts or barns, under the vast open sky crowded with his beloved stars. He accepted whatever food or rest he was given. He won it with his ready wit, his love of everyone he met, his hands always ready to help, his voice quick with songs, and his faith.

His was not a bookish faith. He found God in the adventures of serving poor strangers and of being helped by them. And he found God in the life of Nature; 'droning bees, scent-laden air; slow circling birds, big bellied sails, a shepherd's pipe, an old-time song; laughter, a smile, and a fluttering sigh' (E.P. Dolorosa). Often he must have been cold, dirty, hungry, sick, itching from insects and desperately tired. But, like A.S. Cripps, he found 'the track gave me my lost manhood back'. By teaching faith, he learned it.

GRACE DIEU 1925

After a year as a Railway Missioner Ned was sent to Grace Dieu. Grace Dieu was a training college for blacks at Pietersburg, where the University of the North is now.

Pietersburg lies on the railway line, 194 km from Pretoria, an overnight journey north from Johannesburg. Osmund Victoria, C.R., described the 2½ hour journey by ox-cart on the dusty track from the station. 'The distance is 25 kms. In that space there are just three big veld waves, with a river to be crossed in the trough of each. Great granite hills rise sheer out of the veld with vast piled boulders, at distances from 8 to 160 kms like so many islands in a vast ocean, and one comes on them hour after hour. After two hours of driving, at the top of the last rise, one sees far away a little cluster of huts and whitewashed buildings. It all looks so small and remote, yet at Grace Dieu one can find blacks from all over Southern Africa — from the Cape, Basutoland, Delagoa Bay, the Free State,

Zimbabwe. Only want of accommodation prevents the College from taking far more students than it has.'

Grace Dieu was an extremely happy college. The European (C.R.) staff were unmarried, completely dedicated to the college and its work. Some 50 teachers of both sexes qualified each year. By 1925 20 students and staff had been ordained.

Ned was greeted by the Principal, S.P. Woodfield, with the cheerful challenge 'You won't be of any use but your bishop wants you to mark time for a year'. He took up the challenge, and did some teaching and carpentry. 'One day a pupil in the carpentry section brought me a stool he had made. On impulse I said it could be made better, and drew a design on top. From that moment there was a riot of interest in bas-relief carving.' At the end of the year Sister Pauline, C.R., took over. Proper tools were bought. Carving and sculpture continued there often based on designs worked out and sent by Ned. Sister Pauline left, 14 years later, with her student Job Kekana, and founded a carving school at St Faith's Mission, Rusape, near the Inyanga mountains in Zimbabwe.

At Grace Dieu also the archaeologist in Ned came out. He found some important Middle Stone Age implements now in Grahamstown Museum and at the University of the Witwatersrand. These are officially recorded as from the Pietersburg stone age culture, which before Ned was undiscovered. This was Ned's high point as an archaeologist. The stone implements at Grace Dieu were in lovely pink felsicated lava, soft and easy to carve. One of Ned's colleagues used to 'heave a stone onto my place at table, saying "I thought it might be a Bushman's petrified appendix!"' Ned had other enjoyments as well, and Archdeacon S.P. Woodfield, then the Principal, remembers him lying spread all over the floor reading a newspaper or poetry from the Oxford Book of Verse (e.g. Amiens's Song from *As You Like It*) while the Archdeacon played Gilbert and Sullivan and other light music on the piano.

Woodfield notes the impact of Paterson's carving teaching. 'There are still many churches with some of our carving as part of their equipment. We once carved a whole set of furniture for a dining room, with lovely patterns on the back of each chair. A few years ago, when I was visiting Simonstown, I was asked out to dinner one night and found I was sitting at the very table and chairs made by my students.'

Sister Pauline carried on Ned's work at Grace Dieu until 1939. She used a lot of designs sketched out by Ned but extended the work from simple bas-relief decoration to church furniture crosses. Ned came from a background in which it was sacrilege even to put something on top of a Bible, whatever other use was made of it. So he was shocked when Sister Pauline put his pictures of, e.g. the Resurrection 'on a stool for people to sit on — quite gaily!' Sister Pauline's star student was Job Kekana, a well-known religious carver partly disabled and blind in one eye. She took him with her to St Faith's, and through his relationship with Job Kekana Ned's Grace Dieu influence continued. Kekana's memories of Ned are as follows: 'I first met Ned in 1934 when I was carving under Sister Pauline (who died in 1954). Ned designed plaques for me to carve. He was full of jokes and could draw a portrait of the person he was talking to in a few seconds. Then he'd just toss it to him and walk away.'

Kekana liked Ned for many reasons, one of them simply that 'I thought I was lost because Sister Pauline was a woman.' He loved Ned's simplicity, friendliness, humour, readiness to learn people's languages, dedication, faith and perfectionism. 'Whenever a carver rushed to finish a carving, Ned would say "this is cha-cha-cha" (not done properly)'. He found Ned at times a bit startling, 'We thought he was mad,' but inspiring.

'He gave me courage. I have never been much happier than in his presence. He feared no-one though he respected all. I may never again meet such a noble artist and preacher. He was of the chosen few of Christ, one of the chosen few who illuminate the world.'

GRAHAMSTOWN: 1926 – 27

In 1926 Ned was sent to study Theology at St Paul's College, Grahamstown. Grahamstown is a small city with streets lined with flowering trees. Ned's contemporary G.M. Scott found it 'like a small English Cathedral city set down in Africa.' The College had opened in 1902. On Feb 10th 1926 the Rev. A.H. Cullen, later Bishop of Grahamstown, arrived from England as Warden. Next day Ned arrived, only the 75th student in the College's history and one of the worst qualified academically. The story goes that Ned turned up looking like a tramp with a sack on his shoulder containing all his belongings and followed by a fox terrier. He had a broad grin on his face but refused to settle in until he had inspected the premises and assured himself they were up to his requirements.

Ned's signature in the College register gloriously expresses his character. The writing is flamboyantly artistic, showing a splendid disregard for restraining lines. 'Aberdeen, *Scotland*' boldly shows his pride in his birthplace, and the bold, proud flourishes of 'Naauwpoort Public School' contrast with the delicate, narrow scripts with which his colleagues entered their often far more famous schools and universities. Yet there is a basic symmetry.

Ned's contemporaries included his bete noire, the Senior Student in 1927, J.W. Bradford, and G.M. Scott. Bradford seems to have been very earnest, very intense, and accident prone. Michael Scott, who suffered from a tubercular ulcer, later became an ardent campaigner for black and Indian civil rights, the cause of the Namibian Hereros, and Nuclear Disarmament.

In *A Time to Speak* (1958), Scott describes Cullen and Ned. With Cullen he found 'the gospel story became vivid present experience.'

Ned he describes as 'a particular friend. He had a very positive and often pugnacious personality. He was very original and formed his own artist's conception of other people which was usually highly dramatized, and everyone was expected to conform to his conception of them.' Ned describes Scott as 'our exquisite'. Scott is critical of St Pauls' insularity but notes that the students came from a wide range of backgrounds, e.g. a farmer's son, a customs officer, a tailor and a Jewish cockney. Despite their friendship, Ned disapproved of Scott, saying later 'he will never be happy until someone makes a martyr of him.'

Ned rapidly acquired a reputation for mischief, including Scott among his victims. Because of his ulcer Scott had to spend much of his time sunbathing in the nude. Ned and a friend used to arrange water fights at these times, ensuring that the shy Scott's more sensitive parts were 'accidentally' liberally baptised.

Ned was elected Head Gardener in his first term at the College, took over a writer and decorator of the College's humorous log at the start of his fourth term, and continued with it until he left at the end of 1927. Though officially registered at the College for three years, he only attended classes for two. Apparently he was exempted in his third year because of his special talents and particular vocation to work as an artist with the poor.

His final examiner, who had a wooden leg, remarked 'I often feel out of my depth with his work.' Paterson commented 'His wooden leg should keep him afloat.' Paterson's third year at St Paul's was spent doing practical pastoral, artistic and teaching work in the Johannesburg slums.

His gifts as a caricaturist are apparent in the 1927 St Paul's Log. Some extracts follow.

ST PAUL'S LOG EXTRACTS

Third term, 1926. August 31st: Paterson walked over hill and dale in his hunt for Bushman flints of which he is an ardent collector. (Ned now took over the Log.) Fourth term, 1926: (Sole entry): Bradford lost his train. First term, 1927: Bradford came back a day late. Ellis has been named 'Sunbeam' for the present. After five classes of Greek he surprised the class by agreeing that the Greek of Peter is vastly superior to that of Mark, mentioning that he had arrived at his opinion after a study of the original. Young Shaw is intensely masculine and carries a little girl's books to Rhodes College. He plays rugby, and practises by flinging the senior student (Bradford) around, a practice to be deprecated as we might want him.

At a debate young Hall disgraced the College by giving as a reason for armed intervention in China 'the protection of missionaries', forgetting that Christ has several arguments above the merely physical.

We insert two probable happenings in the life of his masculine missionary (illustrated)
1: He arrives on the mission field accompanied by the three cruisers and protected by marines.
2: With the help of field — guns and swords he builds up an obedient congregation. (Hall later made a career of army chaplaincy!)
21.3.27: The Chronicler cut the Warden's hair. The result showed he is inferior to a barber in finish but superior in conversational staying power.
27.3.27: Ellis considerably worried his seniors by attempting to sing 'God save the King' at a Training College concert.
Scott is undergoing a course of sun-baths in his birthday dress, under the eyes of the college wits, for some internal defect (a

form of T.B.). We expect great things when he comes out of his seclusion.
7.4.27: Paterson specialises in rough houses. He can keep Hall and Shaw in order with one hand.
8.4.27: Shaw has been teaching Hall the Charleston. He ought to be fairly efficient by the time the dance has been obsolete for a year.
18.4.27: Bradford caught his train with an hour to spare. It was 80 minutes late.
16.5.27: Bradford has captured the L.Th. He stood us a cake for tea, having got it on reduced terms on a/c of its age.
21.5.27: Hall's birthday. He dropped the laden collection plate in the Cathedral and was, rightly, paralysed with shame. We are doubtful whether to wish him many happy returns.
30.5.27: Dawson's birthday. He received two telegrams. An ingenuous student asked whether twins had arrived.
The 'ignorance of the clergy' is a parrot cry often heard in this Country. It is particularly distressing to find that ignorance includes theological students as well. Before Martyn came, none of us had ever heard of Wepener, O.F.S. How we have rolled in anguish, bemoaning our ignorance, since everything is done there, and all by experts. Now all our arguments are settled by the 'Wepener Use'. The chronicler is, however, dubious about the place.' Wepener, pop 4 600, is a little town on the O.F.S./Lesotho border. Medieval liturgical problems were settled with reference to the Use, practice, in certain great cathedrals and abbeys in England Sarum (Salisbury), Hereford, York and Lincoln. The Anglican *Book of Common Prayer* is derived from the Sarum service books.
31.5.27: Union Day. Hall and Ellis sported the new flag. Later Bradford was seen, all unconscious, wearing the new flag on his coat-tails. (In 1927 the current S.A. flag replaced one dominated by the Union Jack.)

18

2.6.27: In Retreat. Several days of silent meditation, prayer and reading. Absolute silence. Tea-time (depicted). Bradford keeps his back to the gathering but his face to the food. Shaw, at the door, has been leading a double life. Scott does physical exercises in front of a devotional photograph of a Canon. Hall reads the World of Sport in the *Cape Times*. Dawson smiles seraphically. Ellis sits. Taylor reads Forbes-Robertson, the famous romantic actor and producer. Martyn does nothing — with his usual eclat.

3.6.27: Shaw's voice is breaking. In Matins his voice reached falsetto less than a dozen times, (picture of the chapel disintegrating).

10.6.27: Trinity Term. The members have divided sharply into two groups 1 — Brains 2. — Beauty. The writer is far from good-looking. We have been suffering from drought for some time. The dairies are badly hit. The milk is noticeably thicker.

We measured the capacity of the College cistern, and found by one method that we had 160 000 gallons of water and by another 25 000 gallons. Martyn thinks he had better sell his fishing rod. Bradford has preached his first sermon at the Infirmary. His opening words were 'We are all familiar with the Burial Service'. Dawson suggested he should have gone on 'But if you're not, you soon will be'.

10.6.27: Told by Scott. 'What is the difference between a lady mentioned in I Kings and a woman scholar at Cambridge? One is Abishag the Shunammite, the other is Shabby Hag the Newnhamite'. (Abishag was King David's very beautiful maiden nurse and bedwarmer in I Kings I.)

21.6.27: The College is in disgrace again. The Diocesan School for Girls, an institution just opposite, founded for the incarceration of girls of the awkward age (i.e. 6 – 18) has got a troop of Girl Guides. While this troupe (sic) was practising

tracking, the brethren substituted for an arrow running past the college drive another, which deflected a horde of girls to the front door of the College. (illustrated).

23.6.27: In Mrs. Harvey's Tea-room, Bradford asked for sausage rolls, 'I shay mish, d'you keep shassish rollsh?' She returned with three. Bradford ate two, but the writer declined on the grounds that, though he loved sausage rolls and detested Popish innovations, he did not particularly desire to eat meat on a '*fast-day*'. Bradford nearly fainted with horror but did not have enough money to bribe the writer to silence. 'And so to bed.'

Ned signs himself out with a self-portrait, thistle and slogan Scotland for ever. Paterson's last entry in the Log-book dates from November 5th, 1927. It covers the 25th anniversary celebrations of St. Paul's two days earlier, attended by the Archbishop of Cape Town, twelve bishops, and many others. The Archbishop in his addressed stressed the great adventure of mission, St. Paul's examples of courage and self-sacrifice, and the need for foresight and vision, for an African ministry and for financial and educational independence from the Church in England. In this last, St. Paul's had an important part to play. He urged that clergy and laity, men and women, indeed the whole community, should work together for the Kingdom of God and for His glory.

Paterson noted 'the members of the College could not help but feel that Nov 3, 1927 was a great day in the history of St. Paul's'. One form of lay witness would be shown in the work of Ned's pupils at St Cyprians, Grace Dieu, the two Cyrenes, St. Faith's, Chirodzo, Nyarutsetso and Farayi. Others of the laity such as his daughters Barbara and Margaret and his son Nicholas would do their parts, in the scientific and caring tradition of Abishag, in the medical and nursing professions.

The Log is illustrated with many sketches, which flow through the text. Ned on the whole rejects formal borders and

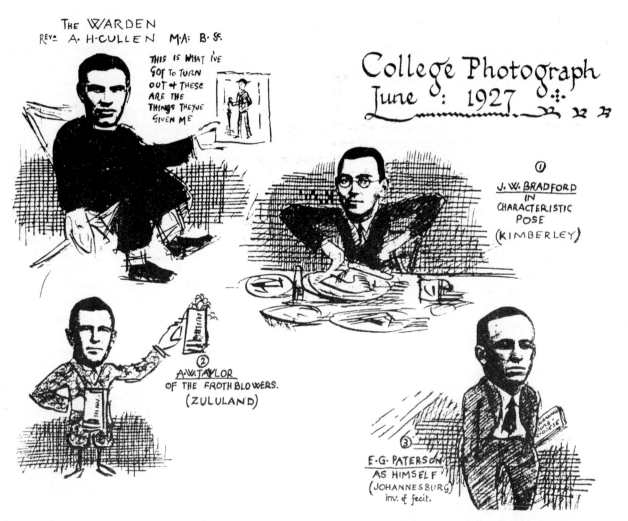

Ned Paterson's self-portrait in St Paul's log book.

Ned Paterson after being ordained deacon in 1928.

Ned taking part in a diocesan conference in Sophiatown (kneeling right).

writes over, round and through his pictures. These are mainly rough sketches of people in action. A popular theme is accidents, real and imaginary, e.g. an ostrich driving Martyn into a thorn-bush, the chapel disintegrating as Shaw sings a high note, and Bradford hanging himself by accident from a staircase with his new L.Th. hood, 'his 101st and last accident with it'. An entire page is devoted to a day of Bradford's imaginary adventures. Late for Chapel he falls upstairs and downstairs (one picture, two inscriptions at right angles, covers both). He is locked in the local lunatic asylum and museum and has interesting encounters with madmen and skeletons. He anoints himself accidentally with sanctuary lamp oil. At tea-time he chants, 'Please pass the jam,' in plain-song. He jabs a fork through his foot while gardening, twists his ankle and misses a ball at tennis. At the end of the day he remains like a cartoon-cat apparently completely unharmed. An ambitious full-page sketch shows a bird's eye view, complete with eye, of the buildings and people as Shaw in vermilion trousers, the medieval colour of lust, successfully chases up a tree and captures the College cat. Ned gravely notes that it is a sober, moral cat 'only on the tiles once last week.' The perspective is curious — there are two vanishing points about 60° apart (the views from both eyes of the bird, its head cocked). The sketches are fun, lively and energetic, but hardly art. Like much of Ned's verbal wit, they suggest and exaggerate rather than depicting accurately, though Ned is a lively caricaturist of facial expressions, and is at his happiest when he puts outsize expressive heads, African-style, on tiny bodies. As is common in African art, every picture tells a story. Sometimes balloons are used in Ned's sketches but usually any needed explanation is given in accompanying text. Unlike the art of Ned's pupils, it is impulsively energetic in execution rather than painstakingly precise, but some of the designs, notably the full-page ones, show signs of thoughtful planning.

A later student at St. Paul's was Gonville ffrench-Beytagh, who also completed his time there in an effective two years (1936 – 7). In *Encountering Darkness* (Collins, 1937, pp. 43 ff) ffrench-Beytagh refers critically to the discipline and, as he found it, austerity of the College, mausoleum-like architecture, the formal ritual and the simple food, especially in Lent. ffrench-Beytagh acknowledges however that a longer stay might have made him a better priest. Ned seems to have responded to the discipline buoyantly. He enjoyed the pranks and practical jokes of College life. He reacted mischievously but sensitively to its Anglo-Catholicism.

He poked fun at the girl-chasing of Hall and Ellis, Shaw's muscular displays, Bradford's accident — proneness, passion for food, and pretentiousness, and Martyn's apparent conviction that his home-village of Wepener (94 km SW of Maseru) was the hub of the universe. Ned's own background was poor enough for St. Paul's simplicity to seem no privation. The lack of luxury helped him to concentrate and to develop his eyes, ears and inner spirit. When his girl came along he would not chase her, like Ellis, on foot, or like Hall on a motor-cycle, but their spirits would grow together with a deep, slow, strong, bold fruitful love.

JOHANNESBURG: 1928 – 31

In January 1928 Paterson was made a deacon in Johannesburg. From 1928 to 1931 he served as Assistant Curate of St. Cyprian's Church, Sophiatown, under Canon Wilfred Parker, a nephew of the Earl of Macclesfield and later Bishop of Pretoria. Parker had the care of all the slum areas of the city. Paterson notes that Parker, in whose house he stayed, was a very cultured but in many ways a very innocent man; who 'couldn't understand evil'. Parker gave him accommodation and £12 a month 'pocket money' in lieu of the diocesan rate of £25 a month. They got on very well together. Paterson notes his amusement at Parker's innocence, 'spending more than half the night watching the cat getting kittens and terribly interested in it all'. But Parker gave Paterson a polish, an understanding of values and manners, which was to be very useful. 'I loved the squalor of Johannesburg, working among the poor, the coloured, the beer gardens, the brothels, with tragedy, poverty and evil walking about in the bright light of day.' The African townships, notably Sophiatown and Western Native Township, now Western Coloured Township, had a vital community spirit. Their energy was ready to explode into merriment or murder at any time. The nickname for 'Western' was 'Thulwndisville, Okay, I Heard You, or The Place where the Houses Talk to Each Other.' The houses were brightly painted with symbolic designs. Ned enjoyed all his work and learned a great deal from it. He continued teaching e.g. at St Cyprian's School, Sophiatown, and decorating churches both with paintings and with relief carvings by himself and his pupils. He also encouraged them to write poetry. Before he left the Rand he had decorated over a dozen churches in whole or in part, and probably a great many more. He claims to have decorated 14 round Potchefstroom alone.

One of his tasks was the decorating of parts of Johannesburg Cathedral, including making a set of designs on the pulpit. They showed the coming of Christianity to Africa. This pulpit was later transferred to the Church of Christ the King, Sophiatown, and when that was demolished, it went to another African church. His main works in the Cathedral were the heraldic emblems of the ancestry of the diocese from Canterbury through Capetown and Pretoria; the cushion caps on the pillars of the nave; and the decoration of the high altar and its baldachino. As the cores of these were concrete, Ned worked alongside Bill Schonken, a foreman plasterer. His tools con-

sisted of kitchen knives and spoons as more elaborate ones were not available.

They worked at high speed because the cutting had to be done before the drying plaster hardened. 'The first cushion cap we made kept the architects' formal design, but I used my imagination and carved the four sides into the Garden of Eden, the Creation of Eve, the Temptation and the Expulsion, and from that moment I had no peace. They said 'Leave the others and get on with the pulpit.' The architect asked for full working drawings but I was rather bumptious in those days and said 'No drawings! I either do the job or I don't! And as Wilfred and the rest of the building committee were behind me, Bill and I were left to do as we liked. It was exciting and absorbing work. I studied photographs and pictures in books of Romanesque sculpture and architecture to get ideas and these influenced my final designs for the pulpit.' The emblems were done next, a day spent on each, then coloured by painters.

The baldachino came next. A baldachino (ch is pronounced k) might be crudely described as a huge erection on four pillars over an altar. It makes the altar look a bit like an old four-poster double bed, but several times the height, with no curtains, and a massive top. There is a tendency for baldachinos to look as though they are defying gravity and could crash down at any time, e.g. on the priest. This introduces a useful element of suspense into church services, which otherwise might become boring.

'Can you do anything with it or shall we blow it up?' Ned decided to go ahead and prettify it, watched over by the architect 'who had probably never seen such a big job done in so carefree a manner.' After plastering, a pentagonal cavity was made. In it the kitchen cutlery made the Chi-Rho of Constantine (which looks a bit like an P under a X) with at the sides Alpha and Omega. These express and symbolise Christ, triumphant over suffering and death, Christ the begining and end of all things (Alpha and Omega), but look a bit like A^X_pW Ned was disturbed to hear an elderly lady say 'it was kind of him to put the Dean's initials (A.W.P.) but why did he put the X?' The four altar pillars were made 'One', 'Holy', 'Catholic', and 'Apostolic' expressing the qualities claimed for the True Church. 'There are a lot of touches of humour in all this carving plus African wild life and medieval grotesques'. The work was coloured black, gold, vermilion, blue and green, suggesting medieval missal decoration; the baldachino pillars black with gold andgilded capitals. This led predictably to controversy — the rest of the Cathedral is almost oppressively austere — but Ned got away with it. The Cathedral was consecrated with a big procession and an elaborate service. Ned, hidden away in the organ loft, looked down and was content. The building council was also pleased; blowing up the baldachino would have been a bit messy.

They gave Ned 50 rands (£25) which paid for a bicycle for his work in the slums. Parker, however, apparently thought the brilliantly coloured baldachino was too ornate, and later had it whitewashed. Around this time Ned became a priest. When he was ordained, his mother said 'Dinna be a priest laddie, be a minister'. Translated into unbiassed English, this meant 'Don't be an ornamental speech-maker. Work with your hands. Sweat for God and man'. Ned never forgot these words. 'I was sure now that I had found my true vocation and was very happy at my work. My days were full.' Even when he was not engaged in church work, he was occupied, sketching buildings, taking photographs, and studying drawing under a Jewish friend, Mr Amschwitz. Ned loved Jews. During this period Ned had also been deeply involved with matters of church finance, a concern which would remain with him at Potchefstroom and Cyrene. With pride he would later note (Diary, April 19, 1953) 'I am very expert on the Jo'burg system of Finance for African Missions. I was very prominent in getting it

started down there. We must give the African laity more dignity and power and set them over the clergy in the matter of finance. Also they must pay more'.

These problems remain serious in 1985. To give up control over finance means to some extent to give up control over doctrine, over ritual, and over what is said in the pulpit, and there are a lot of problems, especially with the richer laity, and with dangers of a politicised church.

Ned's own attitude is stressed in his letters and sermons. Christianity is a practical religion involving an active, personal relationship with God, who is encountered in Churches and other places. A church which stifles the individualism of its members is a dead church. As God loves us for ourselves, we love one another for God within us. Each new member has something individual, something personal, something different to contribute, and a really active church accepts this, perhaps at the price of dogma and authority. Church buildings exist to the glory of God, not man, and serve the living, not the dead. They need not be expensive or elaborate. Church projects should serve real needs, not publicity; and honest faith rather than rich sponsors.

Dynamic African Churches have to accept a Christ as African as the Christ of European churches is European, and as irritatingly individualistic. They have to accept the same fullness of the relationship with Him, and pay the full price, and this can be reflected in architecture, doctrine and ritual.

POTCHEFSTROOM: 1931 – 38

In 1931, Bishop Karney of Johannesburg appointed Ned priest in charge of the mission to Africans at Potchefstroom.

The mission area was large, with fourteen out-stations and some 12 000 members of the Anglican Church. 'I had a honey of an African priest under me, and also a lot of catechists who ministered to the congregations scattered in groups, mainly to European farm areas.' He would spend entire weekends on one out-station, living with people, sharing their food, getting to know them and sometimes painting the clay churches they had built for themselves. His wall-paintings were very popular.

'I found it quite easy to be friendly with people. I was continually in and out of their houses, drinking cups of tea and eating with them.' His success as a missionary was simple. He showed respect for his people as individuals and for their culture. 'I've always tried to leave the African with his self-respect, as he has given me mine.'

Geoffrey Clayton became Bishop of Johannesburg in 1932 and used to join Ned on his outstation trips, living as an African. Things usually went well, but one day Clayton was shocked to see Ned refuse to eat a strange food. 'Geoffrey was angry and reproved me. ''It is food and, whatever it is, I would have eaten it'' (Luke 10.8 'Eat whatever is set before you') ''My Lord,'' I said, ''It is a cow's udder'' and he said ''Oh''.'

Noel Brettell remembers a visit to Cyrene years later. Ned asked Kay, his wife then, what was for dinner. Kay: 'Cow's udder.' Ned: 'Ugh!' Kay then dished up a hillock of mashed potatoes with four sausages stuck in it.

Clayton, says Ned, was 'a great man'. During the tedious hours of synod discussions, Ned drew caricatures of the speakers. Once he drew one of Clayton and showed him it. 'Ow!' said he, 'Now I know why I was always called ''Codfish'' at school.' When he first came Ned welcomed Clayton to the Transvaal with an African choir, but he found Clayton 'a tough nut to crack'. Clayton appointed Ned Director of Missions for the Western Transvaal, still based on Potchefstroom. The area covered was the same as during his Railway Mission job, but with much more administrative and advisory responsibilities, especially towards the African and Coloured communities. Ned was responsible for a flock of 12 000 church members. During this time was started the first Cyrene experiment, brainchild of one Fred Sharman. It was an African communal agricultural and industrial training mission. This project broke down in the late thirties when diamonds were found in the area. The temptation of easy money through diamond picking proved too great for the mission to survive.

MARRIAGE

In 1933 Ned married Mary Phillips, who came from England's magnificent Lake District, with its wild and majestic mountain scenery. She was a Vicar's daughter of the old style, from West Seaton, Standwix, and Troutbeck, home of John Peel in the song. Her life was 'good and dull: small family and village doings; the best food in the world worst cooked; a small circle of village friends; girl-guiding, music, flowers and walks in impossible weather'. She was trained by S.P.G. as a missionary at St Christopher's College, Blackheath where she loved company, jaunts, feastings and the peace of the Chapel. When she left, the Principal remarked cheerfully 'Molly, it has taken me two years to find out that you haven't got a brain at all'.

In 1929 Molly arrived in Johannesburg and joined the workers in the House of Bethany, next door to where Ned was curate. 'I met her almost at once and we looked at each other: she with red cheeks and kinky hair, some cottony thing for her dress and sensible shoes. I said ''You look like a scrubbed butter churn'', and she replied naively ''I did once get a prize for butter-making''.' Her natural innocence appealed to Ned at once. During the next few years, he organised mission work and she ran Sunday schools and Girl Guide groups in the

African areas. Molly was musical. She played the piano and the violin, sang and taught folk-dancing.

'Molly was utterly without pride, very quite and peaceful, a complete contrast to my ebullience. Once she came to me in tears: "I have to make a report to synod about my work, and it doesn't seem to me that I have done anything!" "Bless your heart" I said, "that is easy. You write a report on what you plan to do for the coming year." ' The result was a great success.

Ned and Molly saw a lot of each other, realised they liked the same sort of things and the same people, and finally got married. Ned's stormy strength and Molly's gentleness, patience, innocence and spiritual depths complemented each other. 'Molly was born to bind up and encourage others and to remain out of sight herself.' She loved the ordinary pleasures of life and the joys of nature. There were four children: Mary, Barbara, and the twins, Dugald and Margaret. They were a very happy and united family.

In October 1938, Edward Paget, who had become Bishop of Southern Rhodesia in 1925, invited Ned to start a school for Africans near Bulawayo. Ned accepted, and so the adventure of **Cyrene** began.

Wedding Day (1933)

*Mary Phillips (Molly),
Ned Paterson's first wife.*

Ned with Barbara and Mary (1936)

Molly with children: Mary, Barbara, and the twins, Dugald and Margaret.

Wall painting in the Church of St Francis of Assisi in Venyersdorp. Later Cyrene style is obvious.

Finishing touches to the pulpit in the Anglican Cathedral of Johannesburg. On the right Bill Schonken, an expert plasterer who, as Ned testified, "helped me tremendously".

4. Cyrene

BEGINNINGS

Cyrene was, in part, a product of Paget's whirlwind energy. In 1936 Paget had read the Government's Tredgold Committee report on juvenile delinquency among the white urban population. The report proposed a rehabilitation centre, preferably under church control. Paget approached John Banks, a wealthy railway engineer, Surveyor of the Railways and farmer who had been forced by a fall from a horse which broke his neck to leave his farms near Bulawayo and go down to sea level. Banks's wife, Agnes Foster of a banking family, would be a great friend of Cyrene. Banks had had a stormy relationship with his farm manager, and was quite keen to hand over the farms Collaton and Irene, 4846 ha. or so to the Church. 'Irene' means 'the Peace which passes all understanding', the Peace of God, so this move was appropriate. 'Cyrene' means a 'palisade'.

So two farms and a splendidly equipped farmhouse came into Church hands. Paget was delighted. He launched two projects there. The first was St Pancras Home, named after the boy saint, supported by the government, and initially placed under John Donkin of the Post Office and Toc H. The hope seems to have been to establish a rehabilitation centre of the kind of Homer Lane's New Commonwealth, but for many reasons this experiment was unhappy. The deliquents were lonely and depressed. There were never more than eight, all boys, ranging widely in age. Costs were high, morale low, and there was never enough for them to do. They tended to run away and get into trouble, seeking adventure in scrapes with the authorities. On one occasion they stole a car and robbed the local store. Meanwhile another home was opened in the capital which flourished and was far cheaper to run. One feature of St Pancras which Cyrene would inherit was the Chapel, designed by Fr Baker, C.R. This was a brick building with whitewashed walls and a thatched roof: simple, intimate, and austere, with a plain cross and a flat altar. It took Ned to realise that bright paintings on the walls, inside and out, would cheer the place up. Paget's second project on the farms was a mission centre for rural Matabeleland. This was to be centred on a school with a strong emphasis on practical skills. Basically the idea was the traditional one of industrial missions: to provide skills and some Christian religion, not to create an urban snob but to train people who would be of value in their home areas. Christianity would not be imposed on the people, but would be a part of the ritual of the mission.

Ned found himself initially in charge of both projects. Donkin had returned to his Bulawayo Post Office job when his wife had a child. His successor Paul Sykes had been, Ned claimed, a consumptive do-gooder, an impractical idealist. Sykes had been succeeded by Trevor Stead who served under Ned but, with eight pupils aged from 8 to 19 felt they had to be coached individually. After some time Ned decided that it was unfair on the boys (as well as the local store) to keep St Pancras going. Without consulting Paget, who was furious, Ned approached the Government which on his suggestion closed St Pancras and transferred the boys elsewhere. This also meant that the Government withdrew most of its financial support and the Committee which ran St Pancras transferred some of the £3 000 Banks had given to another project. This left Ned with £2 000 plus control of the two farms with which to fulfil his emerging dream of an educational centre with an agricultural, technical and artistic emphasis. Ned called his scheme Cyrene after Simon of Cyrene, who helped Christ carry the Cross and whom some people believe was dark skinned. 'The name' wrote Ned 'has come to carry in it the idea of hard work, hard work for God, for Africa, for each other, and for oneself.' Simon's Cyrene was also one of the first Mission centres in North Africa. An agricultural centre, it was named after a Greek nymph whose son Aristaeus was supposed to have invented bee-keeping. To help raise funds Ned started producing a series of cyclostyled sheets the *Cyrene Papers* for the Society for the Propagation of the Gospel and other supporters in London.

FIRST IMPRESSIONS

When the family arrived Ned found the little farmhouse magnificently furnished with some Adam and Sheraton furniture. There were wide verandas, spacious rooms, and even electric light, a great luxury. Outside were beautiful shrubberies and flower gardens, with further away plantations of eucalyptus and conifers. Great marula trees shed acid fruit, and there were

monumental wild fig trees, reminding Ned of Christ's words to Nathaniel, 'When you were under the fig tree, I saw you' (John 1.48). Beyond the farmed land were wide-spreading camel thorn trees.

Ned quickly took up archaelogy again. 'I have found an excellent rock shelter occupied by Wilton man over hundreds of years. From a trial trench we have a fine collection of stone implements, ostrich eggshell beads and many other things.' There were rock paintings. Also the skeleton of a little girl wedged in a rock crevice where perhaps she crawled to die. 'There are many ruins, round them querns and mullers, and spear heads and hoes of iron, hard won from the rock, come to light. Clearing a site for threshing we came across an old grave, the skeleton seated upright with its once possessions about it and an earthen pot which had held food on its head.

'There is a strange beauty in our mimosa thorns as one sees them stark and swart against an evening sky, the branches huddled together at the flattened top like wrists thrust against the weight of air.'

Near the farmhouse was a kopje, crowned with the Union Jack. From it a magnificent view opened out, for Cyrene lies on the Great Dyke between the Victoria Falls on the Zambezi and Kipling's winding 'great, grey, green greasy Limpopo River.' To the East are the strange, ghostly Matopos Hills, a national park where Rhodes' grave lies at View of the World.

Ned found the farms a 'fairyland of interest. Quail spring up to startle us. Guinea fowl are busy at the maize. Nearby, abundant pheasants call raucously. There are wild duck in our dam. Small birds flit about like living jewels in the shrubberies. Buck are frequent visitors. In the bush grey kudu pasture, big as horses, with spreading horns. A family of leopards are nearby and have taken two dogs, but keep out of sight. Civet cats seem to be in every tree at night and wild cats lure our domestic cats away to a more exciting life in the bush. Porcupine root at our potatoes and hunting ant bears leave deep holes, traps for the unwary walker. Secretary birds stalk solemnly about and a hawk keeps effortlessly busy. Lions have been known nearby. Cheetah are on the farm, the gentlest of the cats and very beautiful.

There are edible fruits, nuts and roots and in the long grass there are always flowers such as the small blue wild iris and great spikes of gladioli'.

CONCEPTION

Cyrene would be planned, Ned decided, round a great cross cut in the bush with dormitories at the arm ends and class-rooms in the angles. There would be a primary school with a strong stress on agricultural and domestic crafts. In addition there would be a strong centre for the study and practice of art, especially art reflecting the culture of the local people, African art.

The Rev. R. Hambrook notes that at this time none of the African schools in South Africa or Zimbabwe included Art as a serious subject, although small children were encouraged to model simple objects in clay taken from river banks. Drawing pictures, mostly copied from ones the teacher had done, often very badly, on the blackboard was far as some schools went in art. Painting was non-existent. Clay was readily available and in any case children were used to playing with clay at home. Drawing was however an unfamiliar activity, and paint remains (1985) expensive.

The farm possessed a brick kiln and some thousands of bricks ready for use. Ned roughed out his plans for classrooms and dormitories, and a new chapel, on the kopje, and, after a sudden veld fire accidentally cleared the site, building commenced.

'The question of architecture is a thorny one. The architecture of Abyssinia and the West Coast are too cold and brutal. All we can do is work thoughtfully with an eye to Africa'. Typical Ned! He wanted his architecture to evolve as he built.

A builder, James Zwangendaba, was found and the big cruciform assembly hall, Foster Hall, was started. 110 000 bricks later, 90 feet long and 20 feet across the arms, it was completed on St Bartholomew's Day, 1939. Dormitories and classrooms were also built. Ned was sure there would be plenty of students. A small night school he started was very popular, and he noted a passion for English language as the gateway to knowledge and communication (there was little vernacular writing).

Students at the school would pay £4 a year for board and lodging, plus tuition fees. In fact the pupils paid 25% of the costs of the school, the government 50% and private donations the rest.

The St Pancras Chapel was renamed St Peter Ad Vincula, St Peter in chains, in honour of St Peter's imprisoned vision of an angel in Acts 12.7. A famous church of his name in Rome contains Michelangelo's *Moses*. *St Peter's Chains* are celebrated every August 1st in Southern Africa. Ned prepared a new altar for the Cyrene Chapel, embedding in it a lightly carved font stone sent by Fr Osmund Victor from Simon's Cyrene. He put a missal stone carved with the opening words of St John's Gospel on the altar, and behind it painted Christ as an African priest, one hand raised in blessing, the other holding the Sacrament. Round the edge was written: NGALOKO BONKE BAYA KUNANZINI NGABAFUNDI BAMI — UMA NI TANDANA: in English, 'By this shall all men know that you are my disciples, if you love one another.'

About this time war was declared in Europe. Ned was content to wait for instructions from his bishop; at 43 he was too old to rush into battle. But he did see Cyrene as playing a part:

'our spur is a Christian conception of life against the enemies of God's freedom and His Church.'

THE SCHOOL OPENS

The school opened on January 22nd, 1940. 'As the day raced towards us we were forced to think of school equipment, of plates, dishes, spoons and all the things needed for cooking arrangements. We had no idea how many students would turn up. We had placed an advertisement in the newspaper and seventy parents or students had applied. Deducting those who had, probably, applied but very likely would not turn up, we prepared for half that number, one that would be quite manageable and a good deal in excess of the first number of most new schools.

'A mud floor was the final job in the Foster Hall. A team of women came and smacked it down with great flails, singing in rhythm, as they worked. Now we can relax until Monday, we thought, and enjoy two days rest. But all hope of a peaceful weekend was shattered quite early on the Saturday by the arrival of four barefooted students burdened with blankets, their boots — probably the first pair they had ever possessed — slung over their shoulders to save them from damage, all looking a bit scared because they could see the dismay on our faces when they had hoped for a ready welcome. They were the first of a steady trickle that soon became a stream and then a flood.

By every available means of transport they came, noisy groups by train, in twos and threes by bicycle, on foot — looking tired and dusty from a long walk; — the flow seemed endless, sweeping us out of all order and method supplies of everything. And still they came. Only when the Foster Hall seemed to be overfull could we turn adamant and refuse to take more, and by that time our roll stood at ninety four.

Imagine our feelings! Here we were, a school unknown and untried and almost unbuilt, offering — neither we nor they knew quite what — and we were strained to the limits of our space. What HAD we offered that had brought these students, not only from small village schools in the bush, but also from old-established schools run by Europeans? There would be only one answer: we had advertised ourselves as ''an institution for the development of art in agriculture and craftsmanship'' and that is what brought them. The covering letter we had enclosed with application forms had made it clear that we are teaching the crafts even to beginners and not merely from Standard V or VI, the classes which usually include for the last year of a boy's school life, some training in craftsmanship for, say, about two hours a week.

Each had brought blankets. Feeding them was our first concern. I had a good supply of ground maize from our own field. I had three great pots for cooking and there was meat in the larder. Their first question was ''Where are we going to sleep?'' and that was solved by offering them the vacated rooms of St. Pancras for the time being. We then turned to the more pressing question of organisation, of sorting out the boys and putting them in classes according to ability, etc.

We were still talking as the sun went down. By then I decided that we had had enough and asked the teachers to collect the boys for an opening service in the chapel. Standing at the door to welcome them, I heard ''Ah! Ah!'' of surprise and pleasure, at my mural painting of Christ behind the altar. At least they could see art can be done. Ned's technique for fresco painting at Cyrene was to mix the pigment with petrol rather than paint direct on damp plaster. This technique was followed by his students.

There appears to be no record of the days that immediately followed. Later, Ned writes, 'The school's day begins at 7 a.m. with field work for some; for others there is work in the carpentry line. We need a lot more forms and desks. After breakfast they all attend their classrooms. In the afternoon, from 2 to 4.30 there is craft work of various kinds. In the carving class I have six students who show great aptitude and I am concentrating on them until they themselves are able to take each a couple of disciples, so that by the end of the term I may have perhaps thirty boys on it.

"I insist on English as the only spoken language during school hours. They all wanted to learn English. My rule would help them do so quickly." Later this rule helped the pupils to win inter-school debates and other public speaking competitions. In the meantime it helped overcome tribal cliques and speeded up teaching.

The first art classes went well. 'I handed each pupils a loose sheet of paper and told them what I wanted them to do. There was a cry "We can't draw." "Now, just try!" One boy said, "What shall we draw?" "This morning I told you the story of the Prodigal Son. Draw it!" "I can't!" But I let them get on with it.'

SETBACKS

As the months passed, Ned became aware of the first of Cyrene's failures: the climate. Rain in that area is very erratic. As the agricultural side of Cyrene proved disappointing, great stress was put on the artistic side.

By 1941 Ned was having teacher troubles and Molly had cancer. He playfully named her 'Mathambo', 'Bones', because she was so thin. The pupils loved her and pitied her.

1942 was another drought year. At Pentecost Ned wrote "Like a rushing mighty wind". The epistle for Whitsunday (Acts 2.1 – 11) comes home poignantly. For lack of wind we have had a most tragic year. We harvested nothing. As the drought continues, day after day, week after week, month after month, one suffers with the slowly dying plant life. In such a time one grasps one's kinship with nature, with life that looks mutely to man for that help he cannot give. Our windmill is idle. Our vegetables, flowers and crops are dead. For a time all water for our 140 souls had to be carried two thousand metres from the farm house. The air was still. A match, unsheltered, flamed without a quiver.

The bleached dead grass, like a mirror, flung up into our faces the merciless glare of the sun.' The Government had issued emergency rations of 660 gms of maize meal per day, 220 gms short of the normal diet. Sickness was rampant, and many pupils had lost relatives from starvation. There was even a strike of pupils, a gesture of frustration at a seemingly hostile world.

On the plus side, the building students had completed three open-air classrooms, known as *Ndhlovu*, *Ncube* and *Moyo*. Max Davison had joined the school as Principal, taking over the administration. Ned gave himself the title of Warden, in ultimate charge and particularly involved with religion and with industrial and craft classes. A new carpentry instructor came.

The arts and crafts were developing quickly. 'The beginning of a tradition sweeps new students into their stride. Every student draws and paints and they form an appreciative background against modern school-art. A few may become artists and the others will learn to appreciate art when they see it. The growth in confidence is amazing.

We have been exhibiting our work at an inter-racial exhibition of the art of school children, opened by the Prime Minister. The white children used symbols common to all European children and painted in a good school style. Our African artists varied considerably in their approach to their subject matter from the primitive daub, through the purely abstract and on to the almost photographic, and the symbols they use were common to all primitive art.

Cyrene Chapel, exterior view — east end Rondavel. From Left: Madonna and Child; Adoration of the Shepherds; Mary Magdalene and St Peter. Murals were commenced in 1948 and completed in 1951.
(Photo: Mrs J. Spink
Courtesy: P.P.I. Spicers (Pvt) Ltd

Chapel, Interior. Rear: The Last Judgement, John Mhlaba, 1942. — Right: Christ Commissioning the Disciples, Joseph·Ndlovu, 1943.

(Photo: Ministry of Information.
Courtesy: Tourist Board)

Four sculptured figures in Wonder-stone done at Cyrene in 1950/51. — From left to right: Mother and child, Ndebele warrior, man with the thorn, the Good Shepherd. All carved by Sam Songo, except the warrior which is the work of Lazarus Kumalo. The figures are about 12" in height.

St Francis of Assisi carved by Sam Songo in Wonder-stone

35

Our wood-carving was also shown and caused not a little surprise and quite a few offers to purchase. Both the European and the African Education Department are a great help in pushing forward the claims of art to a place in the national life, and I find myself called upon to speak and lecture a great deal. 'In the country of the blind the one-eyed man is King'. I am glad to do this speaking. Art was the means through which faith came to me and I see it as part of that 'life to the full' which was promised by Our Lord.

We are to have forty African teachers of various denominations at Cyrene in the coming holidays for an instructional course in the teaching of art and carving and clay modelling. There will also be a music course with special reference to tonic solfa notation.

The aim of all this fostering of art is mainly the development of a canon of taste by which they may appreciate the work of all artists. Incidentally, it is very evident at Cyrene that the boys most capable in art are rapidly becoming the most capable intellectually, as though the whole tenor of their lives had moved up a peg.

SCRIPTURE

In a scripture lesson (using Scripture as a springboard and not as a roof) something is done to make the pupils think.

The missionary must sow the whole Christ, so far as he is able, even if the consequence is that in their streaming to the light, they should refuse to subscribe to our plan for it. It is God's work to make a man good; it is our work to make him interesting to himself.

ARCHAEOLOGY

Because of the drought, the grass is short. This has brought to light many old native ruins and also prehistoric sites. We now have an excellent collection of stone implements of the main Stone Age periods from the Paleolithic to the Bushman and some record of the Iron Age which the Bantu brought in. This material is useful in teaching History.'

Ned's passion for archaeology was shared with his children and many of his pupils and colleagues. In the isolation of Cyrene it provided an exciting release for pent-up energies and frustration. Like art it developed the imagination and curiosity. The children collected and discussed stones, strange plants, all sorts of things. When blacks were in the party, they were invited to give the African names for things and got an exciting opportunity to practise their English and share the adventures of Ned's own children. Ned was fascinated by the local herbal medicine, though he wryly notes most of the local plant concotions were apparently purgatives!

Ned was deeply conscious of the need to develop an active awareness of African culture and the past. He wanted much more done to develop African culture-music, art, drama and poetry and dance. 'Cultural slavery,' he noted, 'is a poor exchange for a mess of pottage' (material benefits).

Cyrene he felt should aim to preserve the people's pride and self-respect. It was already beginning to influence art in the rural areas. In 1943 he wrote 'Cyrene has turned out students who are continuing their art in their villages, and some of them have written back quite frantically, asking for paints and brushes and paper and chisels. Those lonely artists may give the spark necessary to fire potential artists who have never been to Cyrene and we must have some sort of Group into which we will try to sweep them — and the musicians and poets and writers. Brother Roger C.R. at Penhalonga and E.G. Wyatt of

Hope Fountain write to me that they are both busy about poetry.

Our painted chapel attracts a lot of attention as its walls slowly cover themselves in murals done by the students. The most recent mural is twenty-four feet wide and depicts a student's own idea of the Last Judgment. Over the centre of the west door, Our Lord is seated on a throne. He holds in His Hands an adze and a mealie-cob, and by this twin standard of ''What have you made and what have you grown?'' He judges the world. Scattered over the wall in strange arabesque are groups of working people busy about their village crafts and manual labour or enjoying the relaxation of music or reading or writing or dancing; a priest celebrates in a chasuble and before an altar that Wippoll never knew and, nearby, another priest holds a child precariously while he baptises it. In the far corner a fearsomely-patterned snake guards a pit down which a parcel of nudes fall headlong into decorative flames and darkness. The East end is complete too, with two African Saints on either side of Our Lord. Other murals show the Good Samaritan, The Sower, The Prodigal Son and a few other things.' The absence of a serious Hell is interesting. Ned knew enough about suffering on earth not to stress it. 'We have laid foundations for a new dormitory and hope to start on an industrial block this year. We have a metal work class which uses scrap metal and turns it into adzes, hinges, trowels, knives, casement catches and so on. Some day we may have a blacksmith's shop and develop this side of the work.

Traditional woodworking is well done here; the bowls cut from the solid adze handles, stools and spoons, but carpentry with true wood halts a little, though they are very keen on doing it.

Drawing and painting have made very great advances and run by their own volition.

At the Government's request we had a refresher course for 52 black teachers of all denominations; clay modelling and music were dealt with by Miss Warwick of Tegwani and I had charge of the drawing, painting and woodwork. In the ten days the black teachers experimented with everything.

Our Pathfinders are neat and well drilled and capable. Our veld is the natural home of scouting and everything necessary to their training-even the possibility of danger is to be found on the farm.

There are schools where something is being done to revive the spirit of African music. But there is only one school south of the Zambezi which is able at the moment to do anything about the revival and expansion of native art; and that school is Cyrene, near Bulawayo. The experiment at Cyrene, where art is a compulsory subject, has resulted in the production of art which is more vital and untramelled by convention than contemporary European school art. The capacity for experiment shown by the students is amazing, as one might expect from any new art impulse, and it is clear that for some time to come this freedom of expression will continue, until they find themselves nationally in art and develop a style of their own. Some large water-colour paintings of history are to be bought for the nation.

The traditional African patience and thoroughness in woodcarving has been linked at Cyrene with modern carpentry to produce things of beauty which will be treasured in many a home. At various exhibitions our work has received great praise and, at a recent exhibition in Harare all the exhibits were sold before the exhibition was officially opened.

Besides these more spectacular sides of the work, Cyrene follows other schools in academic work and in teaching the first steps in carpentry, building and metal work. It would be unreasonable to suppose that, with a full programme, we can turn out trained craftsmen by the time they reach Standard VI, but what we have managed to do is to give a foundation in these trades which has enabled the more intelligent students to earn a living.

We also teach agriculture, vegetable gardening and cattle management. Our students know from experience the value of crop rotation, of winter ploughing and of cultivating; they have their hay-ricks and compost-pits, and they know the approved methods of pest control. All this knowledge will go back to the rural areas where it is so badly needed.

The motto of Cyrene is "uKristu uyisikonkwane sami" which means "Christ is the compass span which bounds and controls my life". A character at peace with God and man has a centre from which all labour and effort radiate. Faithfulness to the job is the best form of gratitude to God as well as being the best form of prayer. We ourselves are, as Arthur Shearley Cripps has it, 'flawed windows through which to get the vision of Christ.'

By June 1944 a big exhibition of art, crafts and music inspired by Paget and held in Bulawayo had been a great success. Almost everything was sold before the official opening. This was the first big Cyrene exhibition. Ned was pleasantly surprised at the success. 'Cyrene art is startling enough: an art of surprising pattern and the oddest juxtaposition of colour, but perhaps it provides an antidote to the evenness of modern life.'

Joseph Ndhlovu, a student at Cyrene since 1940, had been accepted as an art teacher at Hope Fountain mission. This made him the first black art teacher in Southern Africa. Ned notes that Joseph created his work from memory. He had done a big mural in the chapel, sculptured heads in wood and stone, cut designs on lino and wood, and painted a series of water colour scenes from history.

It was clear that Cyrene was training craftsmen rather than teachers, to the disappointment of the local schools. Ned however was cheerful. 'I would far rather think of Cyrene as the spiritual head of an army of craftsmen than of an army of teachers,' he wrote.

Sudden rains brought malaria, with many deaths in the country. The children of the drought who came to Cyrene were malnourished and sickly. They rejoiced in such nicknames as 'Skeleton', 'Windmill', and 'Soupmeat'.

Max Davison left, and the Pathfinder Scouts were taken over by Chad Chipunza and Sitelo Gumede.

The other teachers included a Scot, Ian Muir; Nicholas Mabodoko, the first Cyrene pupil to return to teach; Robert Mukome, the building teacher, 'a glutton for work', and the gloriously named Gordon Goliath Xozumti, who trained at St Matthews College, where Toc H started in South Africa. Gordon and his wife Sylvia were proud to have their first baby at Cyrene. Ned arranged four free scholarships for Cyrene boys in carpentry and building at St Matthews. Gordon Xozumti and his family became very close to the Patersons in the years ahead and the Xozumti and Paterson children mixed freely.

MOLLY

Finally in 1944 Cyrene lost someone without whom it could never have flourished, someone whose caring presence Ned felt right up to the time of his last illness, thirty years later.

'Molly was born to encourage others and keep out of sight herself' Ned wrote. 'She saw something to praise in everyone she worked with — a good incentive to people to live up to the good opinion. Her friendliness was open and natural, a quiet liking for all sorts of people. Her natural respect for others prevented her doing anything that would make even a child lose face with its companions.' Molly had a deep spiritual life of her own which gave him strength in need, yet was very practical, making her own clothes and those of their children among many other things.

'She was much used by the students to get at me from behind.' One nickname for Ned was 'My Wife' because he would tell the boys, 'She's my wife, not yours!' They feared his whims and unpredictable rages, but Molly was always calm and gentle however she was teased or provoked. She worked hard and never skipped preparation for anything she did. A true Aberdonian, Ned had married 'a guid worker'.

'If I were to boil down the nearly 400 letters of sympathy I received, Molly would stand out as a sort of yeast working secretly, a permeating influence for goodness, and beauty and all delight, the harvest of which we shall only know when we see things at last in the light of God's eternal truth. 'Blessed are the peacemakers — the children of God' (Matt 59). Each kiss, like Mary's oil of spikenard, is not wasted. Man can escape the Christ shown in efficiency, but not the Christ we show in Love.''

Molly loved the simple things of life and the beauties of the veld, 'though I think that, in her heart, she would have sunk them all in the middle of the deep blue sea for a handful of weeds from an English garden. She enjoyed her clothes, her little bits of finery, our few bits of silver, the delicacies we get in season, a picnic on the veld. She loved having a visitor and especially one likely to enjoy having breakfast in bed and a little mothering. She enjoyed too, the half hours, stolen from her busy day, and spent in chapel, and from her our children have learned to enjoy what they have, without being for ever wanting to rush into a shop to buy relief from monotony.

Well, there it is — so she lived and so at last she came to face death with all this capital in the bank to see her through. She knew in July what was to be the outcome of her disease and also that great pain was likely to be part of the price of her release. After a breast was removed, it was found she had cancer of the spine. She took the news in deep silence and even forced a slow grin while her eyes scanned what was left of her life. Then she set her face steadfastly towards Jerusalem and, while she journeyed, enjoyed to the full, and perhaps doubly, everything that came her way to make life lovely; her children, her friends, her correspondence, flowers from her own garden, the Holy Communion, the Anointing of the Sick.'

Molly made every day a full one, completely lacking in the morbid pleasure of self-pity. She thrust herself into life with a deep drive to spread happiness around her for as long as she could. Ned and the family knew what she valued. Above all, she valued the happiness and mutual caring of those around her far above her own wants and needs. Over twenty years later Ned explained the deep love which unites the Patersons as basically Molly's doing. She loved them to love each other, so they did. Former Cyrene pupils agree. Against Molly's determined gentleness, there was no hope of resistance. She spread love around her like a quiet epidemic.

Molly had one all-important gift — the gift of thankfulness. She learned to focus all her attention, even at the end, on the 80% or 50%, or 10%, or 1% of beauty and joy and love in her life. She treasured memories of lovely things. She even hoarded postal orders received as gifts, holding the loved thought far more than the money.

A glance, a laugh, a smile, a touch, a kiss were things she stored up in her memory and dreamed about. Awake her dimming eyes sparkled with these memories. She fought pain with the memory of happier times. She worked, as always, at living lovingly and helping those she knew to grow in love, one for another. In short, Molly filled her conscious life so full of joy, and love, and inner beauty, that tension, fear, pain and selfishness could hardly find an entrance to her thoughts. Her joys were things she shared with other people. The scent of a flower, the sunset's light at evening on a leaf, a baby's bubbling glee, the flight of a bright butterfly and the song of a lark in an English spring found their expression in her gentle thoughtfulness. And everything, even the 'valley dark as death' (Ps 23 v 4) was welcomed as an adventure with wonder, thankfulness and love.

Such was Molly's spirit, whose simple acts, whose dusting and sewing and readiness to care for others 'exist for ever in the Mind of God'.

The long decline into death, Ned, uncomprehending, said, would have been perhaps easier to bear if she had not been so brave and uncomplaining about it. 'I am in great pain' was, in her words, 'I am a little uncomfortable.' 'We who watched the mystery of her pain, and who, lacking understanding, prayed into the blackness of ignorance, were aware that with her God was working out in His clear Light, some fulfilment of His Purpose for her which was hidden from us. She had written to her mother. ''I am not afraid of death, but there are some rather frightening preliminaries''. But when these came she was given courage to bear them and she was able to turn it all into a piece of very good breeding.'' 'There was breeding in both senses; good manners and fertility. Molly's was a death of the body, the poor cancer-tortured outer shell. She endured suffering gladly and joyfully surrendered her spirit, soaring, as one new-born into the hands of God. Mary and Barbara were present at the end, the beginning of Molly's new life, on September 3rd 1944. She passed into Peace 5 years to the day after the outbreak of war. As her country's victorious army crossed into Belgium, she also in victory crossed a new frontier.

Molly's example of courageous suffering from cancer would be followed 33 years later by her third daughter Margaret.

There was a simple funeral for Molly, the first ever held in the area round the chapel. The grave is south of the chapel, crowned by a simple stone, facing East towards the rising sun. On the face of the stone are the simple words 'Molly Paterson 1898 – 1944'. On the back Ned carved a rising Phoenix;

Molly's spirit, triumphantly reborn, purified from the flame-bred, pain-bred ashes of its former self. There the grave remains today, victorious in its glorious solitude, by the track to Westacre and Bulawayo. Every visitor to Cyrene passes near its silent witness.

Inside the chapel Ned placed a carved stone memorial font. It expresses and fulfils Molly's love in Christ for the children of mankind and asserts her own triumphant birth, washed clean of sin, beyond the grave. Ned carved it with the triumph of Christ's purifying love over the Seven Deadly Sins (Anger, Envy, Gluttony, Greed, Laziness, Lust and Pride). The sins are shown as animals of Africa, except for one, Lust, represented by a man, the only animal, Ned noted, which is always in season!

This baptismal font expresses Ned's own love for Molly, and their shared love of children, of the vital and sustaining forces in Nature, and of God. It tells us of their joy in fertility natural and spiritual. It demonstrates their sense of the tremendous adventures and privilege of bringing the water and grace of self-discovery in God to Cyrene. Resembling at once a chalice and a womb, this carved reddish rock in the form of a corn mortar reveals the artist, priest, teacher, husband and father working creatively in humble partnership with his beloved wife and with his God.

Molly's passing deepened Ned's vision. Confronted with the mystery of her strength, her loving humility in suffering and the beauty of her life, he lost something of his old arrogance. Her journey in a sense redeemed him, for he had to find for himself, and pass on to others that spiritual well of strength which she had found before in prayer and quietness. He learned from her to depend on others and to lean his love on God, like a child on a father, full of wonder. In her passing she was like a child's playmate, gone away to other joys. Looking after her he wistfully inserted in the *Herald* and *Chronicle* her death notice and 'To die must be an awfully big adventure (Peter Pan)'.

5.　"To Please a Queen" (1944 – 47)

NEW LOVES

Molly Paterson's death in the closing months of the War was a great personal triumph for her. For Cyrene and the Paterson family, it marked the beginning of two years of change. Out of the ashes of the old love a new and family unity would painfully emerge. The coming years were to see the greatest of Cyrene's achievements, built on the family's love. Molly's love of her countries, too, would help. Cyrene was to owe much to the sensitive interest of members of the Royal Family. In Ned's conversion to the view that queens are more than quines (ordinary girls), Molly had surely played her part.

Ned was a middle-aged father, with four children of assorted sexes and temperaments. The children had European names and expressive African ones given by Ned. Mary whose Western name means Bitterness or Wished was called Lorata, Love; Barbara, The Stranger, was called Boitunmelo, Joy; Dugald, Dark Stream, was called Matli, the Adventurer, and Margaret, Pearl, was called Kaisho, Peace. Used to running wild, they were children of the veld, natural hunters and explorers, remarkably spontaneous, extraverted, and individualistic young adventurers, but they needed someone to guide and look after them. For the first year or two the solution seemed to be a succession of rather prim governesses, Miss B. and Miss P., priggish, vicarious intruders into the wilderness who tried to civilize the children. Miss B. even tried to insist on the children using finger bowls at meals. Having assured themselves that the governesses were almost infinitely shockable, the girls ensured that they were appropriately shocked. Such sheltered maiden ladies as Miss B. and Miss P. needed an education before it was too late. The unfortunate governesses discovered that life was a daily succession of unpleasant adventures. This education of the governesses was carried out enthusiastically, for they seemed to have a sadistic streak. On his part Ned was unsympathetic to their ideas about training in the virtues of Victorian manliness and delicate femininity. Cyrene was the wrong place for girls to be brought up to sew samplers or to be wilting vicarage lilies. Ned was pleasantly uncivilised himself, despite his love of Chinese art, and preferred it that way.

Nor were attempts to woo Ned himself entirely successful. As with the children the superior blandishments of pseudo vicarage culture fell flat before him. Remarks like, 'Isn't it strange that all the seeds know what plants they will grow into?' were not treated with the respect due to a governess as a successor of Darwin, Linnaeus and Lamarck. Even Ned, still overcome with the memory of Molly's timeless loveliness, was not susceptible to ancient female charms and immemorial wisdom. Parlour conversation such as 'What a pretty picture of the Bristol Channel, my brother met his death there' did not lead to an immediate ardent proposal of matrimony and a honeymoon in that very spot. How strange!

In short something had to be done, and as Ned clearly did not believe in the old Scots saying, 'The grey mare's the best beast', his eyes must turn elsewhere.

The Rev Sydney Smith once asked 'How can a bishop marry? How can he flirt? All he can say is "Come and see me in the vestry after the service".' Ned, though not a bishop, would have normally had quite a problem. What girl would want to raise another woman's family on an underpaid lonely mission station? The answer proved to be a remarkable one: Kathleen Iona Mitchell from Harare, nearly 22 years younger than Ned. In 1936 Kay was one of a party of 25 local school girls, newly matriculated, who were selected to tour British schools. On board the ship were Ned on his first leave, Molly and the two little ones, Mary aged two and Barbara, aged 9 months.

The second night aboard, a Saturday, the Anglican girls only were sent down to their cabins to press their frocks for early Mass next day. A man looking a bit like a russet haired terrier was scribbling away downstairs and said to them cheerfully, 'I'll see you in the morning' and the girls, misunderstanding, chorussed 'Like hell you will!' or words to that effect. Next morning, when the fox terrier — Ned, — conducted the service, there were some pretty blushes of embarrassment.

Kay got to know Ned and Molly well. She loved young children, and adopted Mary and Barbara, allowing Ned and Molly to have a bit of long overdue honeymoon. Molly once borrowed Kay's hockey uniform. The women became good friends. Kay was a bit of tomboy — she still is. Her hair was unruly, much wind blown, and a sporty life did not help. Often she was sent from the dinner table to brush her hair. When they got to London, Ned sent her a brush and comb kit at her hotel and from then on they kept in touch.

About 1942, Kay was secretary to Robert Halsted, a war-time Minister of Transport first in her hometown, Harare, then in his main business office in Bulawayo. She used to visit Ned and Molly at Cyrene, and help with the family. Ned was at this time absorbed in archaeology, gradually beginning to work over the Kopje behind Cyrene in a series of reasonably systematic digs and scratchings. He would continue this with the help of the children and favoured Cyrene pupils until the family left.

At home Kay and Molly, who had developed breast cancer after the birth of the twins in 1938, were good company for each other. Aside from the cancer Molly had worries of her own — the financial worries of a mission run by Ned's head-strong enthusiasm and worries about the health of both twins. Dugald, the Adventurer, had a respiratory blockage, while Margaret Peace, had weak lungs and despite her indomitable personality, would remain prone to illness all her life. Kay's practical enthusiasm for life and driving energy responded to Molly's quiet spirituality. Both responded to and rather complemented Ned's aggressive vitality. And as Molly's illness grew worse, Kay more and more took over the role of a friendly aunt to the children.

When Molly died, Mary was 10, Barbara 9, and the twins 6. Mary had always been very close to her father and had inherited her mother's natural ability and skill with a needle. She was able to do a great deal for the younger children, and Gordon and Sylvia Xozumti helped. But life for Ned was lonely and Kay drew closer to the vortex of need, enjoying his humour and making clothes for the children. Ned got an engagement ring made in Johannesburg. His wooing style was unorthodox. He just produced the ring and said, 'There then, we are now engaged.' They sealed the bond with a kiss. Ned and Kay were married in Harare Anglican Cathedral by Bishop Paget in July 1946. Kay was quickly drawn into the financial problems of the mission. Ned's salary £43, to support himself, a wife and four children, was less than she had been earning as a secretary. She organized efficient sales of farm products from Cyrene in Bulawayo.

CYRENE, 1944 – 46

1944 – 47 was one of development at the school in various directions. Ned employed a local African teacher to teach traditional rural woodcarving with simple implements, adzes, scrapers and scorching tools.

'Siziba makes bowls and other articles. He cuts them from a solid log of marula, a softish wood which does not crack. He has bright eyes and powerful yet sensitive hands. I took him through the house and showed him a few treasures: a Ming ivory, an Indian bull in silver, a 17th century Spanish Madonna and Child in ivory, a Persian vase inlaid in silver, some Chelsea figures, an Attic foot in bronze. Siziba read in an instant what these long-gone artists had had in mind. As he held these things with the hands of a lover, it was clear that he understood perfectly the travail of soul that had been put into creating their work. ''I send my soul through time and space to greet you. You will understand.'' Siziba understands the native method of smelting iron from the ore, and his adzes and other tools are all of his own manufacture, perfectly adjusted to his mind and hand and eye and quite lovely things themselves.

In spite of all the lacks in African village life until the beginning of the century, lacks which included the plough, the wheel, the potter's wheel, squared carpentry — they yet had, hundreds of years ago, in this craft of iron smelting and working, a reputation which brought Arab traders to buy of them the iron which the then world preferred before that of India and Arabia.

Siziba is now at work with a small circle of disciples. He also spends time in trying to master something of the art of decoration.

In December I took my children to the Cape for a break, and included in my luggage a roll of our school paintings, Miss MacCullogh of the Child Art Centre at Rondebosch very kindly hung them on the walls of her school.

The pictures caused very great excitement. I swelled visibly with pride. The pictures next hung in the Parish Hall of the Saviour's Church, Claremont. Finally I attended a meeting of the Fine Arts Commission of the South African Government through the generous help of Miss Ruth Prowse, Keeper of the Michaelis Collection of Old Dutch Masters. The pictures were hung in her private gallery where the meeting was to be held. They remained there for two months and were seen by a great number of people.

About Easter Miss Mary Waters, a lecturer at Rhodes University Grahamstown, about 2 000 km away, visited Cyrene to see our art. She took home a loan collection of paintings and organized a very successful show in Grahamstown. Cyrene has had a year in which I have been the only European on the staff. Possibly I needed this spell of loneliness to give me a purchase of the Life to come. At least I have learned something of the permanence of the mind of God, and also of the extreme rightness and beauty of death.

Though I have been too long in the bush country ever to believe in a kindly Mother Nature — always in the night there are the tiny rustlings and scamperings which tell of the grim seriousness underlying the seeming peace — yet, even so, 17 000 acres of veld have helped me a great deal to get things straight. One looks over an open spread of tall grass which sways restlessly in a tide which comes to no harbour but which breaks up the tawny yellow into softly speaking reds and golds, while here and there from the grass, as if punctuating it with the rightness of music, the great thorn trees thrust up the wrought iron tracery of their bare branches. One must not be misled into thinking, because there is an absence of violent movement, that things will remain just so. There is a faint rustling in a nearby tree and when an ear is pressed against the bole there rise in volume the myriad crepitations of the termites. And one day this tree will crash to the ground to become life of another sort, and yet, because it has existed, because it has been ''said'', one knows that, in the mind of God, this tree will forever stand stalwart against the sky. Visitors sometimes show concern because our frescoes are painted on the walls of a chapel which is no more permanent than are the average buildings in this country; but I am sure that to think that way is wrong. That the frescoes have existed at all is the thing that matters. Their continued existence is quite another thing and has nothing to do with art. Having existed, they too become permanent in the mind of God and in His love and care. That is true too, of a woman busy about the unappreciated drudgery of housework. There is human regret when things pass away. There are regrets for the treasures of our history destroyed in the War. There is an inconsolable sorrow in the loss of a loved one — but for the rest there can be nothing but profound thankfulness for the thing that existed and which has been ''said''.

Mr Gordon Xozumti has taken over the running of the academic work and as he is very expert as a teacher we expect the accustomed proportion of passes at the end of the year. It is a joy to have teachers in love with knowledge who will give up their evenings to study.

The Xozumtis have suffered the loss of their baby Walter and now we have two graves in our little graveyard. But Mrs Xozumti is going to a Training Hospital this year to qualify as a nurse to help other mothers in Africa.'

Gordon Xozumti taught Geography and Ned History. Saddened by the official propaganda which presented all whites as

noble and blacks as barbarians Ned stressed the materialism of the whites and the nobility and the greatness of many of the African chiefs.

It was decided to turn much of the land into a ranch for cattle belonging to the mission. A lay missionary, Mr Midgley from Yorkshire, a carpenter and joiner, was invited out to Cyrene to take over the ranch. The chapel was still being painted.

'Our Chapel has new frescoes. Sylvester Chibayi has done a very large one of the Parable of the Talents. James Ratumi has done 'The Good Shepherd' with a wealth of detail, and the lost lamb is being carefully noted by a hyena, a leopard, a jackal and a vulture, while a native Good Shepherd seeks it out with a grass torch. Only in this fresco did I interfere on one small point which will perhaps amuse you. I noticed that, in place of the lamb which figures in our depiction of the story, James had a most potent looking ram. I got him to change it, but I have since wondered whether perhaps James was not right, for in the human sphere it is not the lambs which stray! Livingstone Sango has done a delightful small fresco of our Lord among the trees and flowers of Livingstone's fertile imagination, and the subject is Consider the Lilies.

Stephen Katsande has done a small fresco of the Martyrdom of St Stephen. A new altar cross has been made in which our Lord is seated, coped and in His Glory in the centre and with the world for a footstool while the emblems of the four evangelists fly out from the panels at the ends of the arms. The chapel is a gay and happy building, with plenty of light to show off the colour. More than half of our students are communicants and others are attending Confirmation classes.'

Despite the harsh times Ned kept his sense of humour. 'Winter clamped down on us and in a few nights we lost almost all our vegetables. Many of our students had never seen the ice before and it caused great wonder. One boy brought me a 15 inch icicle and asked what it was called. I said ''It is called ice, and I will give you a sixpence if you let me put it down your back.'' He took far too long to get his shirt clear of his belt.'

Archaeological work had gone on fast. 'We have now perhaps a ton of stone implements from the veld, representative of the cultures ranging from palaeolithic to that of the Bushman, also a long list of Bushman paintings, We have quite a collection of the iron pottery and beads of the early native peoples. The study of these things is very rapidly becoming an exact science. It is the living things that throw our ignorance into high relief.'

Ned was worried about race relations. Many of the R.A.F. men who had gone back to Britain had taken with them crude prejudices against the Africans. Ned notes 'The African people have been loyal subjects of His Majesty both at home and e.g. in the African Rifles at war. It is worth keeping their loyalty by helping them to retain as much as they may of the fruits of our triumphs and blunderings.'

1946 was a successful Exhibition year, starting in Bulawayo. 'The City Hall was a splendid setting for the 120 large pictures which lined the room to form a background for our handwork in the centre; the great Cyrene chest, carved furniture, decorated wooden bowls and small carvings in stone and wood and stucco. By closing time the second day a solid mass of whites, blacks and Indians milled round it.

There were two very important factors in the success. We took to the Exhibition six students to work at pictures, starting with blank sheets of Whatman paper. All through the Exhibition these boys were surrounded by a crowd of onlookers. The reactions of white children to these artists was amusing because they started arguments with the boys, and just would not believe that the pictures they were doing were their own work. A scrap of paper was produced and drawn on and at once came the request ''Will you do something for me in my autograph album?'' After that the boys got no time to do their work and more than 80 albums were contributed to. It was good to see the way in which all sense of racial difference disappeared and friendly chatter took its place.

The other factor which helped a lot was a collection of 1460 drawings and paintings from students' drawing books pasted into three huge scrap-books. These drawings show the whole process by which the boys have achieved their results — the primitive drawings of beginners, the wild experimentation, the struggles to master technical difficulties. There was not a moment when those books were not being looked at, especially by our own refugees from Europe.'

Sir Humphrey Gibbs tells a story of this Bulawayo exhibition and Ned's impetuous vitality. 'I went in about two hours before it was due to open, to see if I could help get things arranged. I found the hall completely empty. Ned only arrived half an hour before Lady Tredgold and the public. In those thirty minutes we pinned up about a hundred paintings and arranged the woodwork on tables'. Ned got away with this sort of thing because the effect he was trying to achieve was one of a kaleidoscopic richness of colour and variety of forms, rather than any basic harmony or sense of peace and order. Contrast the slowness and deliberation with which the work on Cyrene Chapel, still far from complete in 1982, was carried out. Lady Tait and the Bishop insisted the Exhibition travel to Harare, the capital, 480 kms away.

'Here again the Exhibition was a very great success. While Lady Tait was opening the exhibition, one of the small boys I had taken up with me to work at the show was busy slicking in at great speed the interlacing branches of a great tree, and while all eyes should have been on the speaker, an awed group round this boy gazed goggle — eyed at his amazing dexterity.

With the Zimbabwean exhibitions over, the stage was set for taking up the offer of the South African Association of Arts.

The Exhibition was set out at the Argus Gallery. The lift to the Gallery was kept busy for the entire fortnight of our show and the liftman told me that we had broken all attendance records except one. But that, he added confidentially, was Mr _____'s exhibition and he only paints nudes.

The second show was held at the Child Art Centre at Rondebosch where the children from sixty-six European schools saw the pictures. There was a third show at Pietermaritzburg, Natal and then the exhibits, slightly battered, were returned to me and now await re-packing to go to England.

The only snag about all these shows was that they were for Europeans, and the few blacks who saw them came in by accident. That is a great pity. Recently, a Johannesburg newspaper held a competition in Art for black youths. Four of our boys entered their work. They gained three first prizes and one second prize.

The wall space in our Chapel is now exhausted by the addition of five murals: The Woman of Samaria, The pearl of Great Price, The Treasure hid in a field, The Call of Zacchaeus, and The Healing at the Pool of Bethesda. We must now turn our attention to the outside walls of the Chapel.'

The Midgleys had finally arrived and settled in. William was very jolly, with the build of a quarter-master-sergeant 'but mercifully a couple of inches shorter than I'. Winsome was a trained nurse, especially in gynaecology, which didn't prevent her from drowning a batch of tom-kittens and keeping a female.'

'The Xozumtis left Cyrene in distress for Gweru after Sylvia had lost two children. After a student strike had been curbed and three teachers dismissed, the Xozumtis returned with their latest child, Sylvia, later a playmate of Nicholas Paterson.

The strike led Ned to some bitter remarks about education and his pupils. 'It is Monday on a cruelly hot day: the classroom thermometer shows 90 degrees at 9.30 a.m. and Standard IV are struggling with a test in Arithmetic. The walls of the classroom are white by intention but spattered by the boys who smear fresh cow dung on the stamped earth floor on Saturdays. The inside buttresses are soiled at hand height by skylarking boys who have taken corners at speed. The corrugated galvanised iron roof creaks as it expands after the cool of the night. On trestles stand ink-spattered tables, and seated at them are forty-five boys.

The genus 'small boy' is much the same everywhere in external behaviour: those without handkerchiefs sniff periodically; there is a muttered — eight sevens are . . .; a head clutched in agony over a knotty problem; a hand waved at a fly; a clicking of rulers; the rubbing of corny soles against itchy calves; the scrape of nibs against inkwells; the smell of ink and paper and cowdung and humanity.

This picture of an unmanageably large class, multiplied many thousands of times, is very typical of what goes on all over the Empire, and of all these schools perhaps 90% is in the hands of the Church in one or other of its forms.

What is the urge which crowds our schools? I have, in the past few months, been setting as subjects for compositions a series of questions designed to discover what is in the minds of our students as being the aim of life. The answer, I found, depends upon the control maintained over their passions and desires. About 90% are frankly unashamedly out for an easy life and easily earned money, with motor cars, girls, food and drink, and the strumming of a guitar never far away. Of the rest perhaps 8% are curious about things and places and desire to travel or to know how things work. The remaining 2% recognise that there are other people in the world and that we have a duty towards them.

Very possibly these percentages will not be vastly different in England. In the minds of most of our pupils is the idea that by attending school they will be able to earn more money, and perhaps a paper certificate which will fix the lowest figure it is possible for them to earn. There is no love of learning for its own sake, no curiosity or puzzlement about human relationships. To this type of student the idea of universal literacy is abhorrent because it would destroy their pre-eminence over the illiterate. As one small boy remarked ''When I have completed, I am going to be a parasite because my people are fools''.' Further Ned felt the 'diploma disease', learning for a piece of paper rather than for wisdom, resulted in a sense of frustration, bitterness, envy and growing hatred, especially as it was often confronted with selfishness and silliness on the other side. Ned was opposed to the colour bar, which restricted certain jobs to whites. It created on the one hand a genuine sense of bitterness against the protected lazy European worker. It also gave an excuse to envy the worker who in fact deserved his success.

'Few of us have entered into our heritage.' Ned was against paternalistic colonialism. 'We cannot be by birth alone, the inheritors of the Kingdom of God — these states of being must be entered into (see Matt 7:21), and if only we had entered into them none of the troubles which flock about us would have come to birth. We are certainly not two thousand years ahead of the blacks, as some people say, but we have armed power, organising ability, business acumen and inventiveness, and it is by virtue of these and not our culture that we control them.

'We must on our own accord, resign ourselves to the grim fact that, in the Empire, we are not a Christian civilisation; neither truly Christian in the sense that we have overcome fear by love, nor civilised in the sense that our treatment of subordinate people or even our teaching of them has profited from systematic or wise thought.'

The problem of materialism runs through the Cyrene papers, but no satisfactory solution is proposed. It reflects a basic human tendency to measure merit in terms of possessions. In traditional African society the measure is in terms of cattle,

wives and children, etc. In modern urban society this is displaced a bit towards a nice house, a big car, clothes, radios and so on. The magpie instinct which leads one to collect and accumulate things is a form of this. The accumulation of marks at school, good conduct badges, collections of coins, stamps, stones and other worth-while childhood pursuits build on this natural tendency and can guide it to more lasting values and concerns.

The contrast between the standards of living of the white and the black and the explicit desire of the latter to develop the lifestyle of the former made the whole problem worse. In 1948 Ned compared pay scales on the South African Railways with those on the Rhodesian ones. The South African track foreman (ganger) earned £18 a month and his labourers each earned about £7 a month plus generous rations. The Rhodesian equivalent were nearly £50 a month and £3 a month plus rations. 'The native is prone to reduce his food to the point of undernourishment if he has to feed himself, so that he will have more money to spend on other things.

My own black teachers do not spend more than ten shillings per month each on their food. They all have shiny bicycles costing about £14, watches at about £7. One has a camera at £5, another has a pair of binoculars at £6. They all have nice clothes — not for school use but for going to town — and it is because of the desire for such things that they will never be satisfied, whatever salary they get. I have only one teacher who buys a newspaper or books to read.'

Possessions Ned felt were accumulated for display as 'Status symbols' not for use.

Ned's other pet concern was about the careless borrowing of things, especially tools. Again this reflects a widespread human tendency to waste, e.g. government, property 'because they can afford it'. Respect for property is something usually learned at home. At Cyrene it was sometimes hard to appreciate how costly and how easily damaged imported metal cutting tools such as chisels and files were. The problem remains with us. In Ned's case, it earned him his famous nickname. The one kind of misconduct which made him really angry was carelessness with tools. Then his rages exploded like a tornado — anywhere — even in Church during a service. The instrument of vengeance used for corporal punishment, he claimed, was the penis of a buffalo, carefully dried out in the sun. It served the furnace of Ned's waiting anger behind his twinkling eyes. He used to joke 'Remember, I am not called Matokhwane, Cannabis Rage, for nothing.' His pupils respected him the more for these occasional outbursts. They knew he was right. Those who chipped hard-to-replace costly tools damaged everyone in Cyrene. Carelessness hurt Cyrene as a whole. Because care is hard to learn, carelessness went on. At the end of his time at Cyrene Ned claimed his efforts there were 'like fighting cottonwool'. Perhaps he forgot that each generation of boys learned something from his care and even from his rages.

Cyrene had had one important and lively newcomer in 1946.

SAM SONGO

Sam Songo had joined the school, one of the most remarkable of the many handicapped people to pass through it. He had been found living a miserable existence in his home area of Mberengwa by the School Inspector, Jimmy Stewart. Sam, like many of the handicapped, combines an alert, highly intelligent and sensitive mind with acute physical deformity. His legs are completely withered, and his right hand has two serviceable fingers. 'Jimmy brought Sam to us. His car drew up. I saw him help out what appeared to be a helpless creature who lay on the ground, and I said "Oh Jimmy! What is the use of him?

48

What's the good of him?" And Jimmy said "I think his left arm is nae so bad".

We had a little baby chair — a sort of big doll chair — and Sam was put in this — to his great delight and wheeled away to become one of us. Sam slipped easily into our routine.' He felt he was wanted and there were things he found he could do, especially when it came to painting in water colours. He would be found painting when the able-bodied were otherwise engaged. Sam soon showed that he could carve. People like Sam brought Cyrene its international fame. Sam's alert mind, fertile imagination, acute observation and patience made him an excellent artist, carver and painter with his left hand. Like many disabled people, he turned his disability into an asset, developing senses which remain underused in the rest of us. He is modest and gentle, and sees his art and his Christian faith as reflections of the same experience. Like Ned, he uses his art to explore human experience and finds his faith explains his experience. He fiercely denies that there is anything 'un-African' about his art or his faith. He uses art to help other people on a voyage of discovery. For him, art has led to a deep faith, a deep Christianity. Both were developed in contact with Ned Paterson at Cyrene.

Sam nowadays teaches woodcarving at Mzilikazi Art Centre, Bulawayo. He is the proud father of seven sons, who share his independence of spirit and his love of mankind. Within a few months of his arrival in 1946 he was already a great success within the Cyrene community.

A ROYAL VISIT

In 1947 the Royal Family visited Southern Africa: King George VI, Queen Elizabeth later the Queen Mother, and the Princesses Elizabeth and Margaret. Ned had previously been introduced to the Duke of Windsor when as Prince of Wales he had visited South Africa in 1925. That meeting had slightly cooled Ned's republicanism, but he still had little time for royalty, and seemed to feel the Kingdom of God was too much ignored by the worldly powers. He repeatedly points out that there were missionaries in the area half a century before Rhodes came. Well over 90% of formal African education was done by the churches, yet this work was largely ignored officially. 'Very wisely' Lady Kennedy, the Governor's wife, arranged an informal exhibition of mission pupils' work at Government House. Ned sent up the first great carved Cyrene Chest a wooden chest carved with historical scenes and emblems by Cyrene pupils, some carved plaques and Calvaries showing strong derived influence of Eric Gill, and some pictures painted by pupils.

Ned and Kay went up to Harare. Ned was immensely amused at the vast prices being charged for clothes to be worn at an evening reception to meet the Royal Family — off the peg dresses priced from sixty guineas up to three figures, shoes at nine guineas, etc. Ned returned to Cyrene to find an invitation to a similar reception in Bulawayo. His solution to the dress problem was practical. He had his one dark suit cleaned, repaired and pressed, and bought a cheap set of miniature 1914 – 18 medals which he promptly christened Pip, Squeak and Wilfred. Kay solved her dress problems by simple process of borrowing an evening dress 'a concoction in silver lame' from a friend.

The reception started late, after fireworks, with Ned amused at the peacock splendour of the guests he knew so well in their drab everyday clothes. 'How nice you look, Kathleen' said Frank Roselli, a friend. 'It's borrowed,' boomed Ned cheerfully. For the rest of the evening Ned and Kay commented 'It's borrowed' whenever the other praised anyone's finery or appearance. So everything from jewellery to handbags, shoes to

hair and poise, eyes, teeth, scent and smiles could be gently mocked with this one phrase. Ned was given little chance to praise beautiful women on this evening, anyway!

The National Anthem was played. 'First into view came her Majesty the Queen, all a twinkle with precious things, her crinoline swaying gently as she took us all into her smile. She seemed the embodiment of grace and courtesy. I had a catch in my throat. His Majesty the King swung out to confirm an appointment with Sir Godfrey Huggins. For a moment I stood next to the living core of Empire and heard again the slow deep voice we had heard in the Christmas broadcasts through the War.

'I felt a touch on my sleeve and heard Lady Kennedy's voice. ''Her Majesty would like to speak to you''. Before I had time to remember I was married I stood before the Queen and heard her completely shattering words, ''I am coming to Cyrene tomorrow''. In terror over our complete unpreparedness I searched at once for a way of escape. ''You *can't* come! Our curtains are all torn.'' ''I do not mind that'' ''But our boys will all be away at the Matopos Indaba and there will be nothing to see.'' The Indaba, a gathering of the people to meet the Royal Family, would be held eight miles from Cyrene, and the boys had to walk there.

His Majesty came up. ''Why can't the Queen come to Cyrene?'' he asked gruffly. ''Transport must be found!'' So that was that. Kay meanwhile had heard with sinking heart the word ''tomorrow'' and prepared herself.' Unfortunately Kay and Ned had lent their teasets, teapots and tablecloths, all wedding presents, to Mr and Mrs Childs who were to give the Royal Family tea next day. Even the children's christening bowls had been lent them as sugar basins.

The Queen put the Patersons more at ease by chatting about a Calvary she had chosen from the Cyrene exhibits in Harare. This carving, by David Chituku supervised by Ned, showed the crucified Christ as a beardless young African with both the Virgin Mary and St John as skin-aproned and nearly naked Africans. Kay and Ned found a helper in Audrey Sly, described by her husband Sam as 'two lengths of satin stuck together', who lent them tea things.

Ned and Kay set off home. They were in for a disturbed night. When they got back to Cyrene they discovered that Mrs Midgley, the carpentry teacher's wife, was about to give birth. So Ned turned round, ferried her the 30 km to the hospital in Bulawayo, and finally returned to Cyrene at 2 a.m.

At 6 a.m. Ned heard Timothy, the house servant, stirring, and got up. 'Timothy, the Queen is coming here this morning'. 'Wow!' The boys promptly shifted the furniture into the garden and cleaned the house before breakfast.

The phone rang. The King had arranged for army transport to take the boys to the Indaba. The boys were impressed. One was heard to remark 'A European king does things for other people. Our kings want us to do things for them'. Breakfast over, teachers and boys were distributed to demonstrate all Cyrene's activities.

'The great moment approached. There is a car!' sent me scurrying out, to find Audrey with bread, a teaset and an armful of flowers to decorate the drought-stricken garden.'

At 11 a.m. distant dust showed the pilot car and the lovely sleek Daimler which carried the Queen. Her Majesty greeted Ned and Kay, and Ned took her to the Cyrene Chapel. She was concerned about the thin drought-starved cattle she had seen on the way. The chapel, showing the whole development of Cyrene art, impressed the Queen and the Press. Ned enjoyed it all 'it was said none of the photographs would show me with my mouth closed'.

The party went up the hill to the carving shop, where the boys were busy carving and painting pictures. A small soapstone carving of a goat suckling a kid was greatly admired. The boys asked permission to give it to Princess Margaret, whom they felt had been rather ignored. African folklore teems with sympathy for younger brothers and sisters.

There followed visits to the carpentry section under Mr Midgley and to classes in English (Gordon Xozumuti) and Arithmetic (Austin Mynanda).

Then the school bell was sounded. All the 110 boys assembled in the form of a V shaped choir. One of them carried a large Union Jack. They sang their national song Nkosi Sikeleli Africa — God Bless Africa.

Then Sam Songo was pushed forward in a child's wheelchair. With his left hand he presented the Queen with a plaque of an African Madonna and Child, carved in plaster by another disabled pupil, Stephen Katsande.

After tea the royal car left. The army lorries took the Cyrene party to the Indaba. 'One of the boys said afterwards, "We saw the King, we saw our friend again, and we saw the Princesses". That was what we all felt. Someone had come to visit us, and had gone away, our friend. Next day the royal train southbound for Cape Town and home,' was slowed at Figtree. Ned handed up to Peter Townsend the plaque for Princess Margaret. Hands were clasped, a 'God bless' shouted and the train picked up speed and was away.

'Let me sum up in a story the feeling awakened in many hearts by the Royal visit. A Jewish friend, who had survived three years in Dachau concentration camp near Munich said to me "I am from Prussia. I know what is meant by aristocracy. So I said to myself, This thing is not for you. You should take your dog for a walk. But everybody was losing their heads, and I thought, I shall go just once to see them. Mr Paterson, I went again three times that same day. She is not aristocracy, she is a Queen, just a Queen.'

And the boys?

Timothy: I wonder why the King didn't come too?

Caxton Kandiero: Oh no! The King has no time to be an artist: he has too much work to do about the laws of the countries.

Timothy: But the Queen isn't an artist, is she?

Caxton: Perhaps not, but she has the heart of an artist.

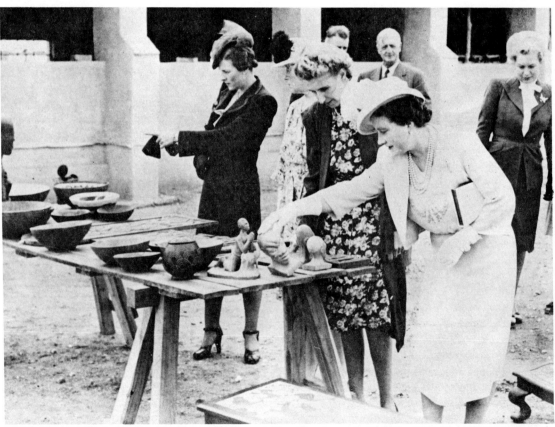

H.M. Queen Elizabeth, now the Queen Mother, visiting Cyrene on April 15th, 1947. Next to the Queen, Mrs K.I. Paterson.   *(Photo by courtesy of the National Archives, Harare)*

6. Triumph: 1947 – 1953

CYRENE LIFE

Stanley Nyahwa, former Director of ZBC's Radio 4, now with Belgian Radio and T.V., is a well-known priest. He went to Cyrene in 1944 at the age of nine after a year at Chibi School, because his father disapproved of coeducation — there were no girls at Cyrene. When he went to Cyrene he was still too young to do agriculture, but could pluck fruit. Though everyone did art at Cyrene, he stresses that it was really developed to give the cripples something practical to do to support themselves. Other gifted pupils like himself might receive special treatment but only with the Royal Visit of 1947 and the exhibitions around that time was any effort made to develop Cyrene as a school or centre for art.

Nyahwa has many memories of Ned and the family. One of Ned's nicknames was Hoto or Kuare (hoopoe) because his hair stood up on end like a hoopoe's crown when he was angry and after it had been cut. Ned's sudden outbursts of anger were swift and soon over. 'It didn't matter what he was doing. He would even come away from the altar and wallop us'. Francis Chindondo, cit Wall, claims Paterson could expel a boy for in- attention or even dismiss the whole staff in a rage, but by next day apologise; boy and staff would be reinstated. The rages con- tinued even in the 1970s but nobody minded for they loved him too much. Ned's ever present tobacco pipe also contributed to his nickname of Matokhwane, a Tswana word meaning, 'the rage which results from smoking too much cannabis.' Another nickname was Madala, old man. Kay, in those days a very

slender girl, was known as Tambo, Piece of String.

Nyahwa was exactly Mary's age, but most of his time at Cyrene Mary was at boarding school. He, Caxton Kandiero, Livingstone Sango, and a few other boys romped around with the younger Paterson children. They went with them on sketching expeditions, botany hunts, and on archaeological hunts and picnics. Ned expected them never to be idle, and was vehemently opposed to the enforced idleness sometimes thrust on them by the notorious governesses. Once Nyahwa horrified his mother by turning up at home with entire sackful of stones, dubiously identified as 'bushman implements'. Ned encouraged the young people to enquire about and explore everything.

Ned's key quality was his love of sincerity in other people. 'He taught us to accept ourselves as we are, and other people as they are. He showed he was convinced of the value of human life. He had an air of reverence for human life which made him for us, a man apart.'

Ned laid tremendous stress on this mutual respect and lived the values he put forward. Cyrene because of Ned, and St. Patrick's Mission, because of Fr R. Adams, another volatile and energetic humorist, produced many priests from their pupils. 'Ned was an extraordinary person. He couldn't be ignored. I heard other people, I *experienced* Ned. And that was sufficient. I like to feel that in many ways in my work I have tried to emulate Ned.' Sam Songo says much the same thing.

But surely there are many areas in Nyahwa's life which Ned and the priesthood have not influenced? Nyahwa has been a school teacher, a political journalist, a commentator on African affairs and on British industry, and a television personality as well as a priest. 'I'm a media priest, a priest in the media, whatever I'm doing.' Ned felt much the same. Once you have stuck your neck in a dog collar, only God can take it off, and he is unlikely to want to do so.

But there were other sides of Ned, he was rather innocent in some ways. On one occasion two of the boys, about to get together with girls, smoked too much 'Miglia' root. This was said to be a potent aphrodisiac, but too much knocked you out, and the boys were found in a coma. Mr Dube, the Assistant Head, was told, understood and referred them to Ned who gave them a medical check up, found they were all right, imagined they were faking sick to get off work, and beat them silly for pretending to be sick when they were not. Next day in chapel he told this story to illustrate the 'need to be prepared for problems but not too much'. The boys roared with laughter. Ned had a passion for playing practical jokes. Mary remembers when they were at Potchefstroom, having horrible injuries painted on her and being sent to Molly to observe the effect. At Cyrene, April Fool's Day was a risky time to be in Ned's way. Once he sent a boy who could not ride, by bicycle (the boy promptly fell off) to Westacre Station to collect non-existent mail. Or he would bark 'There's a draught. Go and shut the gate!' and howl with glee if anyone obeyed. One prank was to order boys to take eggs on teaspoons to the Midgleys at the farm a mile away without dropping the eggs. There were many others and as the children grew up they got ever more involved in April tom-fooleries. When Nicholas was christened in 1948, Ned and the children took Barbara's doll, painted it a bright mauvey colour, purple, black and blue, says Mary. They displayed it carefully wrapped in blankets in a hooded cot in the place of honour on the verandah at Cyrene. While Kay cooed 'isn't he too sweet!' they warmly invited their adoring friends to come and look at Nicky. Visitors retired with fixed smiles or thought up hurried excuses!

Paterson's example was infectious. Of April, 1st, 1953 he wrote 'the day has not dawned before I have been dragged from bed. A newcomer holds in a saucer two eggs which he thinks I have ordered. Eggs are fivepence each, so I take them, replace them with a little dry maize meal, and send him to somebody else. On the Bulawayo road a boy holding a plate of wood ash passes another carrying the school bell, both urgently needed by different teachers. Miles away in the bush a boy trundles a squeaky barrow, searching fruitlessly for a teacher who has broken his leg. Boys stand at Westacre Station for hours before dawn to greet parents who are safe in bed hundreds of miles away. Boys lie groaning on the ground: I gave them a dose of quinine instead of aspirin. A teacher looks sick after trying to write with a carefully prepared waterlogged chalk.'

Ned and his senior colleagues used April Fool's Day as a kind of initiation process for new boys and new teachers. The pupils either enjoyed it or learned to put up with it. Many initiation ceremonies are far harsher. And jokes helped release tension. Sometimes the boys tried to play practical jokes on Ned, but they rarely succeeded. These fooleries were a valuable safety valve from the serious side of life on a mission short of money and ravaged by drought and periodic minor epidemics. Life was harsh and a priest who was at times a bit of a Lord of Misrule was fun to have around. Nyahwa contrasts Cyrene's joy and enthusiasm, its occasionally clowning Christianity with the dour, cold austerity of his earlier Dutch Reformed Church upbringing. Dutch Reformed teachers forced the pupils to commit vast stretches of the Bible unthinkingly to memory and regurgitate them in examinations if they wanted to continue with their schooling.

Religious life was lived as well as studied. At Cyrene, as

before at Potchefstroom, there were times for the boys to put on plays and songs of their own. Children love a bit of drama, and the Cyrene children, family as well as boys, loved the chance to dress up and put on airs. Everywhere Ned's gusty enthusiasm came into play, even at inappropriate times. The Patersons slept on the open verandah of the farmhouse and Mary remembers one thunderstorm in Molly's time vividly. The water was pouring through the roof and ceiling and the ceiling was coming down but while Molly rushed around getting beds indoors, Ned calmly stood aside, taking photographs. Cyrene, in short, was fun.

LONDON SHOW

Through 1947 the drought continued. There was no rain at all from mid-February to late November, when the rains gradually came.

Water-rationing was introduced in Harare. Through the country people queued for water, cattle died, the land was laid bare. But the 45 m deep borehole at Cyrene did not run dry, and the school survived.

In October Ned sent off four cases of Cyrene art to Gerald Streatfield at the S.P.G. office in London: 210 large watercolour drawings, two cases of woodcarvings and painted wooden bowls, plus three scrapbooks holding 1 400 pages from the boys' own drawing books. As the cases were sent off, he hummed to himself 'Speed bonny boat like a bird on the wing', the Skye Boat Song. The song was inappropriate. In February, Streatfield cabled. Where were the cases? A frantic search found them still at Cape Town docks. Then another snag arose: British Government 200% Purchase Tax on all works of Art. Ned was stunned. Britain was spending millions of pounds on

aid to Africa but refusing to exempt from tax the products of a tiny primary school.

The Gaumont Film people spent a month at Cyrene and made a film called Pitaniko for S.P.G. starring Sam Songo. A Central African cripple, accused by a witch-doctor of causing a severe drought escapes being sacrificed in darkness caused by a sudden eclipse of the sun. He drags himself to Cyrene where he is accepted into the Church. Sam enjoyed making the film, which promoted sympathy and respect in the UK for disabled people. But it did not include a solution to Ned's exhibition difficulties. Lady Tait announced that the show would be held in Foyles Bookshop in June and July. But this was not to be.

Finally, it was arranged to show it in the Royal Watercolour Society Galleries in Conduit St, in January 1949. Ned's fears that oil, or steam, or sea-water might have flooded the cases were set at rest, and John Dixon of S.P.G. arranged for the pictures to be exempted from the 200% Purchase Tax. Ned felt the exhibition would serve three purposes: to raise funds for Cyrene, to show S.P.G. supporters something of what the missions were doing, and to offer African art to a London audience. Ned wondered at this time what future Cyrene had. Would it become a Secondary School, a Training College, more of a Technical Crafts School, or a Homecrafts Village teaching pottery, weaving, and embroidery and other skills to black women and girls? Few blacks had even seen Cyrene art, though Cyrene's skills were gradually filtering back into the rural areas. Ned also believed ardently in education for women, to boost the economy. 'I think it was Dr Aggrey of Achimota who first said, "Educate a man and you educate an individual. Educate a woman and you educate a family", and the truth of this saying is very evident when one comes to handle children from homes where the mothers have had some education.'

So Ned favoured the third and fourth options. Unfortunately, events were to make Cyrene adopt the first.

There was another distraction at Cyrene in 1948 — on July 3rd a squalling little bundle of bubbling fun joined the family, in the form of Nicholas John. Nicholas would have an almost completely African background until the family left Cyrene in 1953, for his youngest siblings were 10 when he was born, and his early playmates were therefore all black. This led to some amusing incidents, as when Nic, aged 3, decided to have a birthday party without telling his parents, who were out. Ned and Kay came home to find a mass of local children swarming through the Cyrene farmhouse eating everything Nic could open or dislodge. It would also help him later in life as a medical student and doctor, for he found an unusual level of ease with black patients and they with him. Nic and Ned would have the same sense of adventure, readiness to do without needless luxuries, and to get their hands dirty if there were a job to be done, the same generosity, humour and belief that it is not who you are but what you do for others that matters in life.

Ned set off from Bulawayo for London on Dec. 20, 1948, travelling by train to Cape Town. He stayed with Dean Michael Gibbs 'A completely lovely person, very kind, very gentle, seeing others as wonderful people.' They saw a Nativity play with a very vocal live baby as Christ, and Ned helped decorate the Cathedral crib.

On Christmas Eve he sailed for Southampton on the S.S. Athlone Castle. He conducted the Christmas services. Dr Fortes, a lecturer in Social Anthropology, invited Ned to give a talk at Oxford and was very excited by Sam Songo's work. Travelling by train from Southampton to London 'a great wave of affection came over me for the lovely grey misty landscape — here and there the rubble of bombing — houses paint peeling, plaster cracking off — but I loved every moment of it.

'My whole being went click click as London slipped into place like a much loved friend'. He was greatly impressed by Elsie Fox's arrangements. He stayed with the 'very terrifying'

Leonard Browne, Molly's uncle, and his charming wife Violet (later Lady Le Gros Clark). Their daughter Elizabeth, an anaesthetist, was 'a lovely person'. Ned spent his first evening discussing race relations in Africa, the USA, and England with Dr Kleinborg of the U.N. and others. Later he wandered the London streets, 'drinking in million scenes, so pleased with everything it must have shown on my face' and exchanging warm greetings with strangers.

On Jan 17th Ned, John Dixon, Elsie Fox, Juliet Prouse and Lady Tait met to hang the Cyrene pictures in the RWS Galleries. Conduit Street had been heavily bombed, and had many 'teeth' missing. The Gallery was attractive and efficient. After hanging there were interviews with the *Times* and *South Africa*, and Ned wandered round the local antique shops. 'Living in fairyland — afraid that Kay will suddenly kick me in the ribs and wake me up'. Though the Queen was too busy to attend the opening, she hoped they would use her name for publicity. Ned was thrilled.

On Tuesday, opening day, he wandered in his new suit and dog collar on foot to Conduit St, via Westminster Abbey, bookshops, and a busmen's shelter. At Conduit St, he found Clutton-Brock of the *Times*, Bishop Furse 'looking like an old mud-turtle', and Lady Tait in 'very theatrical widow's weeds'.

After formal speeches the informal chatter of the exhibition opening began, with the usual oddities, 'Far too many wanted to talk about themselves — one old thing about her elastic stockings and another about her false teeth and one wanted to know if I knew her son in Burma.' Ned declined S.P.G. invitation to speak on the same platform as Michael Scott, his St Paul's contemporary, as he 'disagreed with Michael on every point.' He felt Scott's methods at that time were too political and too disruptive and, like A.S. Cripps, felt the rural African's life 'more complete' than ours. A lively evening at the Brownes' followed with Dr (now Baroness) Edith Summerskill, 'a snappy ginger with a touch of Gracie Fields'. The critics responded well. 'Leonard had said, "if you get a photograph in the *Times* it is a great honour" and there on the back page there were three.' These were one of boys making wooden bowls, Zimangalo's carving of A Young Girl and a painting by Willie Nyati. Press notes included the following remarks:

'Original and distinctive. No trace of outside influence' (*T.E.S.* 25.12.48) 'A strange and, particularly in painting, highly individual art.' (*Times*, 12.1.49) 'Surprisingly impressive.'

The youngest boys, *The Times* noted, painted much as English children who had been allowed to paint as they liked, but the older ones painted complicated arabesques, often with an intricate, elaboration of purely linear decoration, the subjects mostly being figures in landscapes. The exhibition 'suggests the spontaneous growth of a new and perfectly recognizable tradition.' *The Guardian* (7.1.49) noted of the 120 pictures 'Our Lord is always depicted as an African. One carving of the Holy Family in wonderstone shows the Virgin Mother and St Joseph as Zulus.

'In a picture of the Epiphany, the Wise Men are Native chiefs who bring mealies, ivory and a hoe as their presents.'

The religious periodicals also stressed the Christian philosophy of Cyrene. 'Christ is the compass span which bounds and controls my life . . . there is a basic unity in all life and life has meaning when we recognize that unity' (*Church and Home*, Jan 1949). 'Put Christ in the centre of your life so that all you do will be like drawing a circle round a firm pin" (SPG *Oversea News*, Jan 1949 quoted in *Sunday School Chronicle*, 12 Jan 1949, cf St Augustine's 'God is a circle whose centre is everywhere and whose circumference is nowhere'). The *Church Times* and *Catholic Herald* commented on the treatment of the subject matter of the religious paintings. In the *Catholic Herald*, (Feb 4, 1949) Iris Conlay described Ned as 'surely a bit of a genius', and commented on the 'very charming literal quality of the work with its intricate and subtle style. Thus St Christopher, a popular figure, is always shown up to his shoulders in water; the Prodigal Son leaves home in a college blazer, and the Good Samaritan resembles a modern commercial traveller. She enjoyed Livingstone Sango's 'Wise and Foolish Virgins' in which the wise ones have acquired wonderful clothes but the foolish ones are naked to the waist. This style enabled the students to identify themselves with the characters. Ned was rebuked by a student for showing the Prodigal Son's mother greeting him. 'So, Sir, you do not know who would have gone to prepare food?' The *Church Times* was more analytical. 'This admirable collection' of paintings of intricate design 'is completely different from the Negro tradition. The artists have filled their spaces with intricate and sometimes brilliantly coloured designs. Among the carvings is a statue of Our Lady and the Christ Child that reveals how foreign and false must European statues and drawings be to the African worshipper.'

The *Church Times* also quotes Ned on art as a 'training in manual dexterity'. 'If one of our boys becomes a waiter he will be less likely than the next fellow to drop the souffle down the diner's neck' (14.1.1949).

The critics noted the lack of perspective, the intricacy and the naivete of the art. Some were struck with its similarity to Indian art and one — 'W' in *The Guardian*, 21.1.1949, noted resemblances to work by Robert Hichens and Eric Gill. David Divine, in the *Sunday Times* (23.1.1949) noticed 'a gusto, a joyousness in the sheer possibilities of paint, the simple piety of the sculpture like early English carved oak, and the direct tenderness' in the Christs and Madonnas. 'The Canon burns with enthusiasm' (*Daily Telegraph* 12.1.1949) 'One of the freshest shows for months' (*Birmingham Gazette* and *Northern Echo*, Yorkshire. 'Obstinately successful' (*Reynolds News*,

16.1.1949) 'A surprising exhibition . . . an outstanding tribute to Canon Paterson's ability to evoke the African soul . . .' (*Guardian*, 1949) The *Illustrated London News* devoted a page to the wood and stone carvings of Adomech Moyo and Abiathan Zimangali, Annet Sambana and David Chituku and another to paintings (by Sango, Ratumu and Katsande), bas reliefs (two by Katsande, one by Zimangali), and the murals at Cyrene. (15.1.1949) The *Tatler* (26.10.1949) cheerfully commented 'some of the Chelsea boys are obviously ripe for the skids'. The *Recorder* (22 Jan, 1949) noted the 'technical dexterity' of Katsande's work, John Balopi's 'sombre, brooding' quality and the deep sincerity of Sango's work. The reviewer was particularly impressed with the 'extra-ordinarily high level' of the woodcarving. David Divine in the *Sunday Times* (23.1.1949) refers to Cyrene's work 'among the most remarkable of the new things of Africa.'

Art News and Review (12.2.49) hailed 'The foundation' of 'An African school of painting' (p. 7.)

The religious and African papers were enthusiastic. Thus *African World* headlined an article by B. Glencross. 'The school with the idea — Cyrene, where Young Africa is Finding its Soul' (Jan 1949), and *South Africa* (15.1.1949) proclaimed the work was 'a beginning in a completely new direction'.

Visitors included artists such as Feliks Topolski, who became a good friend, politicians such as Tom Driberg and members of the Royal Family including the Duchess of Gloucester, the delightful Princess Ramsay whom Ned found most knowledgeable about art and the very matey Princess Alice who chatted about her love of kippers. Queen Mary came, praised the work of Sam Songo, Livingstone Sango and William Mariwi and bought a picture by Sam for the Royal Needlework Society. The Queen bought one by Adomech Moyo.

Ned's conversations ranged widely, from ¾ of an hour with Queen Mary to an encounter with a lady of the night, 'a more than attractive whore' whom he blessed near Hyde Park Corner. Formal lectures included talks at London University and at Leeds and a television talk on 'In Town Tonight'. 'I was one of the sights of London!' Ned was also able to make a quick (10½ hour) visit to his Aberdeen aunt and cousin Maggie in Hamilton Place. 'My aunt very Scotch and I became as broad Scotch as the best of them.' Breakfast was 'four fresh herring, baps, oatcakes and butteries'. Ned and Maggie hunted out a Fair-Isle jumper and blarneyed it from two young soft-spoken Isles folk in a wee fish-scented shop in a wynd by the docks. Then back to London.

Though the exhibition toured widely, Ned was only able to visit one more opening, at Birmingham's RSA Galleries, at which he spoke of the great need to expand education for women and girls in Africa. The *Birmingham Mail* (8.2.49) noted the sense of freedom in the Cyrene work in which houses might float on tree-tops, warriors seem giants, and trees, plants and animals were woven into colour symphonies. In general, at this point three things were reasonably clear. Cyrene's emphasis on freedom in art had produced some striking works especially from the more mature pupils. The most generally praised works were the sculptures in depth, followed by those pictures which were either unusually decorative or translated Western themes into an African imagery. But the danger of imposing one's own ideas on the pupils was great, even if, like Ned, one tried with all possible will to avoid it. Another problem was also apparent: the exhibitions existed to raise money for Cyrene and were not doing so readily. To a great extent the trained artists would also depend on European patrons to sell their work or pay for their skills. Could Cyrene, by stressing art as a social and spiritual exercise and an exercise in training fingers and senses avoid stifling the personal and artistic growth it sought to produce?

Part of the problem bedevils most if not all artists: highly original work tends to make people uncomfortable. The common buyer prefers the commonplace. To produce significant art requires much will power and patrons with discernment who do not domineer.

In May the exhibition was shown in Peterborough, in June in Harrogate, and July in Leamington Spa. In December it went to Malvern and Cheltenham, where it was described as ''the most important exhibition of native craftsmanship to be organised in the last quarter of a century'' (*Glos. Echo* 18.10.49). The *Malvern Gazette* (2.12.49) mentioned the freshness, delicacy, rhythms and unity of the designs, and the rural sense of humour in most of the pictures. The exhibition continued to tour British galleries for several years, and a further exhibition was sent to New York (1953 — American Museum of Modern Art). American interest in Cyrene art was stimulated by a dancer, Barton Mumaw, who air-freighted £170 worth of pieces to the U.S. Tourists from all over the world were also stimulated by a big permanent display of Cyrene work at Livingstone Airport in Zambia, while in the early 1950's two pictures were commissioned to hang permanently in Rhodesia (now Zimbabwe) House in London.

In February 1949, Ned visited his Central friends, the Fittons. They told him their war memories. A Dakota had crashed in their garden. Another Central man, Fossett, an American, had visited them. In an air raid he stood still, glass in hand, enjoying it. 'Gee! this is great!'

On Feb. 14th Ned flew home by flying boat, scribbling as he went. 'All France lies below me: fields with bomb holes, patches of wood, red-tiled farms; mountains crested with snow like a bride and a string of virgins, yellow ochre villages huddling fearful of the frowning granite above them; a terreverte river; the Mediterranean! An American task force, 10 ships, hobbles along at speed below us; Sardinia — red mountains stained with forests rise out of the kingfisher blue sea. Etna — I looked down for a quinquireme with slaves at the oars, — Cyrene, Alexandria, the Nile dark to port and dim, the pyramids, beautiful erosion patterns, green-velvet fields, mud villages, white mosques, palms, Luxor; Khartoum; patterns of tracks and anthills like foliage on a damask tablecloth; Lake Victoria an earthly paradise, hills, houses and palms hung reflected on the lake against dark jungle softened by mist; a kaleidoscope of green with rivers and small lakes; interminable bush; ahead a dark line of vegetation — the Zambezi; a low swoop right over the Falls — touchdown.' He got a lift home by car.

MATURATION

Between 1949 and 1953 the work at Cyrene continued to develop. Cyrene Art went on permanent display at Livingstone Airport in Zambia and a lot was in private collections in Europe and the U.S.A. — Adomech Moyo, a severely crippled polymath, had become the first African teacher of occupational therapy in Southern Africa, teaching arts and crafts to disabled men, women and children in hospital in Bulawayo and running a small school in his spare time. Livingstone Sango, the artist, had turned artistic taxidermist with the National Museum. William Mariwi was a school teacher and very successful religious artist in the rural areas, and many people came far on foot to see his work. James Ratumu had entered a poster competition intended for whites only and received a gift of £20 in lieu of, and bigger than, the first prize. Randford Sililo from Livingstone had done three big murals on Livingstone Museum. Richard Rachidi from Malawi was soon to become the first qualified African Art Teacher in that country. Lazarus Kumalo, a stone carver crippled in both legs and one arm, was producing promising work. Four new murals had been done on the outside walls of Cyrene Chapel. On the South Wall there is

Adam and Eve by Randford Sililo. In The Thanksgiving of Noah after the Flood by Richard Rachidi, Noah appears clean-shaven, elderly and very guileful, naked except for a skin sporran and with a ruptured navel. He stands at a rude stone altar, giving thanks in a drowned world, and through a rainbow in the background the Ark lies anchored.

John the Baptist by Zebedee Chikowore, 'a cadaverous John stands at the end of the South Wall Scheme, preaching irately to the Old Testament characters, while all about him and the rocky desert landscape is a collection of huge and terrifying insects, off which, his preaching done, he is no doubt going to make his lunch.

On the North Wall a great muscle-bound St Christopher strides through calm, fish-infested water against the background of a native village.' Ned was also pleased to note that two former head-prefects, Matthias Dhlodhlo and Eli Ncube, had been chosen as Cyrene's first two candidates for ordination as priests.

In April 1953 an African Festival of the Arts was held in Bulawayo, with Drama, Dance and Music. Sam Songo won the Silver Trophies for the Best Work of Art and for Sculpture. Annet Sambana won the Silver Trophy for Painting. Cyrene pupils also took 17 First Class and 10 Second Class awards.

Richard Rachidi, the first Cyrene artist to use depth of field, and Chrispin Chindongo had completed their Teacher Training and returned to Cyrene to be trained as the Government of Malawi's first Art and Craft Teachers. Their job would be to instruct teachers-in-training to encourage and develop existing crafts, and to revive forgotten crafts and develop new crafts in primary schools. Richard later taught for Ned at Nyarutsetso, and is now back in Malawi. Chrispen, later, the U.N. representative of Malawi, has settled in the U.S.A.

In 1984 ties were announced between Bulawayo, the centre nearest Cyrene, and Ned's beloved birthplace, Aberdeen.

DEPARTURE

After 15 years, Ned felt it was time to leave Cyrene. They advertised for an artist-priest to take over. 'I want to leave because I grow old. A younger man can better earth the bumps and shakes of mission work. Most probably I am a returned empty. I have enjoyed the work very much indeed. I am grateful that my children have had the veld and Africans as their background'. Moreover, Ned found that his government grant as an uncertificated teacher with 5 children was so low that it kept Cyrene in debt.

Finally, after many delays, the Ffrancon-Joneses arrived and Ned and Kay left Cyrene, which went through a difficult period of transition. At one stage in 1957, it consisted of three co-educational schools: a Lower Secondary under R.A. Ewbank, a Central Primary, and a Local Primary, the whole mission under the Principalship of Ffrancon-Jones. In addition there was a group of disabled people, taught art by Sam Songo and David Chikutu. It was a stormy and difficult time. There were personality clashes and the morale of the school declined. By 1958 when Fr Ffrancon-Jones resigned, it was recorded that 'lying in various cupboards and boxes are the broken and incomplete parts of an enormous quantity of tools'. Perhaps inevitably, in response to the seen needs of a secondary school, more formal art teaching was introduced, and too rapid expansion left the mission heavily in debt. Ewbank, now Canon Ewbank and Dean of Bulawayo, stayed at Cyrene as Headmaster and Principal for 22 years, many of them years of war. In that time he and his colleagues pulled the school out of the red and turned it into one of the leading secondary schools in the country. A sound classical scholar, he laid great stress on qualities of Christian virtue: tolerance, kindness and integrity. By 1970 Cyrene was academically tenth among sixty-six secondary schools in the whole country. It was not entirely unscathed by the violence of the times. One night in 1962 a drunken youth, for a dare, set fire to the Chapel. Though the timber and thatch roof was destroyed, by good fortune the murals were unharmed and friends raised funds for a new asbestos under-roof. In 1978 Cyrene's exposed position led to its transfer to Burnside, Bulawayo, as a day school for a couple of years. During eight months of this time renamed Fort Godwin the Mission premises were occupied by members of the Guard Force who behaved as very bored soldiers sometimes will. They were overcrowded — 800 people in an area designed for 300. The Headmaster's bedroom became the officers' bar. In 1979 – 80 George Turnbull took over at Burnside. In 1980 – 81 with Independence the school returned to its old site under Mr Eunice Osman. At the end of 1981 the Rev Neil Pierce, a New Zealander trained at Mirfield, took over the school from Mr Eunice Osman and Canon Ewbank and once again there are plans for expansion and development. British, Ugandan and Canadian staffing helped. One Canadian passed into Peace.

New paintings are being added to the chapel murals, e.g. Solomon and the Queen of Sheba, by Macmillan Sansole (1982). But by this time Paterson's influence and achievement have extended far beyond Cyrene, and the term 'Cyrene art' as popularly used has very little to do with Paterson. Cyrene art, in the popular sense, means art produced in a rather cold imitation of earlier work done at Cyrene, partly because the landscape of the mission, its trees and rocks, makes such imitation convenient. In such a sense 'Cyrene art' was the very thing Paterson with his enthusiasm for life, passion, love, energy and imagination wanted to avoid teaching.

At Cyrene itself by 1983 there were 167 students doing art under Ronald Wollett, who noted their strong preference for non-representational work. The Cyrene students were also transforming the layout of the school grounds to make a link between art as a formal subject and as applied to real life. (*Chronicle*, June 27, 1983). In 1984 the school had 410 boys in Forms I – IV with expansion to Form VI planned by 1986. 240 boys were doing art, with 10 candidates for 'O' Level, the first in the history of the school. Sponsored walks had raised $2 700 for drought relief in 1983 and 1984. The school runs adult literacy classes. Agriculture is again compulsory as in Paterson's time. As Fr Pierce notes, the wheel has come full circle.'

Creative writing, music, traditional and western, are also encouraged, as is a social conscience, expressed in various ways. The school is trying to live up to its current motto LUCEAT LUX VESTRA, Let Your Light Shine (Matt. 5.16).

7. Completion

LONDON LEAVE

The Patersons left Cyrene in August 1953. Ned was well aware that the new art could not remain isolated in the rural areas. He realized that like local music, this art must become urbanised and influenced by the stress and tensions of city life. He was also aware of the need for state patronage if the art was to be effectively developed. In 1952 a Board was set up to establish a National Gallery, and Ned joined it. In August 1953 Ned and Kay went to London on leave. They took with them some packing cases of Cyrene art — paintings in watercolours and poster paints, sculptures and carvings in wood and stone. After some weeks as guests of Mrs John Banks in Victoria, they moved to Chelsea. Here Mary joined them and worked on the classification of African birds at the Natural History Museum. Ned staged a Cyrene exhibition at the Central and was made a Fellow of it and of the R.S.A. He travelled around lecturing on mission subjects and gave a half hour television talk.

While Kay attended classes at Pitmans in commercial subjects, Ned joined the silver-smithing class at the Central. First gilding metal, he went on to work in solid silver. He produced a silver chalice and paten, and a sugar basin and spoon.

At tne end of his leave, Ned was posted to Harare, first to the suburban parish of Hatfield and Waterfalls and then to the Cathedral as curate.

At this time the Arts and Crafts journal *Studio* published a thoughtful and thought-provoking article on Paterson's work at Cyrene by the well-known critic, Anton Ehrenzweig. (*Studio*, Vol CX LVIII, No. 738, Sept 1954 pp. 80 – 83). The paintings from Cyrene, Ehrenzweig noted, combined the boldness and apparent ease of infantile art, aesthetic discipline, chromatic splendour, delicately interwining shapes, and a delicacy of line reminiscent of Paul Klee, whom Paterson acknowledged as a favourite artist. He examined the interaction of aesthetic and realistic concerns, defending the practice of, e.g., placing trees 'above' houses in the sky on aesthetic grounds. He argued that the spontaneous growth of art at Cyrene resulted from 'sudden contact between a native civilization with Western culture'. Paterson could not have prevented the impact of Western art at least in the form of text book illustrations, but he diffused it, and prevented it from smothering his pupils' self confidence. Ehrenzweig compares the communal atmosphere of Cyrene with that of the Bauhaus, both permeated by the 'tension and excitement of continuing discovery and invention'.

He realized that the Cyrene adventure could not be repeated though a number of similar adventures developed in schools of art in other parts of Africa. He stressed the uniqueness and variety of the Cyrene community — Paterson's own personality with his great variety of experiences, and the amazing range of backgrounds of the pupils, meeting and cooperating 'in a common venture of artistic discovery', of self-discovery and the discovery of a common idiom of expression through art.

Ned plunged back into work and writing. 'Every human being starts with an artistic reason for being alive. 2% are true artists', he wrote. (*The Rhodesian Artist*, p. 13). 'Art existed in a common language at Cyrene, as a normal human activity.'' For a genuine art to exist as at Cyrene it should be a communal effort for the artists to express themselves — their comment on life, on what they feel and see in this strange city life, in a sympathetic environment. The people 'do not need art teaching, but simply the tools of art.'

CHIRODZO

Soon after Ned arrived in Harare, the Archivist Vivian Hiller fixed up for him to teach art in Chirodzo School, a primary school in Mbare Msika. This job was for mornings only, and the Church readily agreed. At Chirodzo Ned found that he was to teach art to boys only, from Stds III to VI, perhaps 250 in all.

Chirodzo was a new government school, staffed by, superintended by, and paid for by the Government. The Government was accepting more responsibility for African Education, which had formerly been largely in the hands of churches of various denominations.

At Chirodzo Ned found a well-stocked store of art materials, got together by a man who had never had the chance to use them. There were several hundred tins of poster paint, and boxes of watercolours — and plenty of drawing books, poster paper, brushes, pencils. 'The pupils I had were far younger than I had had at Cyrene — the children of City Africans — so the age range was between nine and thirteen and as such, a different problem. For perhaps a month things went slowly but even in that time there were some who rose clearly above the ruck and on these I capitalised — putting their work on show for the others to see. Soon the idea caught on, together with a greater understanding of the problems set by the art media. Again I chose boys whose work showed a gift of all over pattern and entrusted them with the poster colours and presently I had their work pinned all round the walls to add colour to the art room.

About the same time we started to get visitors who came often from overseas, to see an African school in operation and of course to see the art. The work of the young boys got great praise, as well from the press as visitors and we decided to send to America a consignment of the large 'Paintings by African School Children'. Finally after many exhibitions it was given to the Smithsonian Institute, Washington, who themselves organised exhibitions.

At the start of Chirodzo I decided that some sculpture must be done. I still was without Rhodesian soapstone, so again I imported Wonderstone from South Africa. But there came a windfall of stone. The Imperial War Graves Commission having decided that the graves of all who fell in the war must have a headstone of Portland Stone cut and lettered in England, many tons of these headstones came to this country and of them five tons were broken in transit. I got hold of this and found there was plenty of workable stone in the five tons''. Chirodzo's name means 'to be sharpened, as a spear', a good name for a school concerned with sculpture and carving as well as painting. Here Ned found two great differences from Cyrene pupils: the Chirodzo boys were much younger, and they were city-bred. Ned called them 'the little Coca Colas'. There were much more of simple expressionist pre-puberty art which shows the child's world as an extension of his identity. There was much less patience — the readiness of Cyrene artists to spend months on a picture, delicately painting in each leaf on a tree of a thousand leaves, was lacking. There was much greater European influence, through comic books and advertisements with their stress on intense, instantaneous, and often violent experience. There was much more awareness of violence in life generally, and much less of the quiet things, the spiritual depths, the beauties of nature. An article in *Concord*, Apr. 1956, pp. 20 – 21, by Robin Holmes, mentions phases in the art — crude drawings of suns and birds; landscape paintings; semi-abstract pictures with nightmare forms and pictures of huge animals laughing in a sinister way. For the price of freeing the city child from rural fears was a deepened cynicism about human nature.

'The town child of Chirodzo is a city child, having a whale of time in going about the city and seeing what is going on. He caddies at golf and plays it well himself. He watches horse-racing and all sports, goes to the circus, gambles a bit and sees all grown-ups from the back-door, with amusement, for he sees them without their masks. I asked one which of three candidates for parliament I should vote for. He answered, 'Well, Father, accepting that all three are crooks, I think X may be the best in future'.

Despite the success of an exhibition of nearly a thousand Chirodzo pictures in San Francisco and other successes, for example a representative of Liberty's in London bought some posters for fabric designs, and Americans had the same idea; Ned was unhappy there. His day classes of exuberant youngsters were on top of him for 5 hours a day, 5 days a week, enjoying themselves but tiring him. They were 'too young to make a lasting impression', though he showed great enthusiasm for their work. Art workshops for adults, held one evening a week, were more satisfying, especially in sculpture, and he wanted to develop work in coppersmithing and silver.

NYARUTSETSO

In 1961 the Government decided to establish a new Art Centre at Nyarutsetso, 'to complete or adorn something'. Nyarutsetso was in Highfield 10 km from Mbare Msika. By this stage the National Gallery, opened in 1957 under its ebullient Director, Frank McEwen, was well under way, and a massive International Congress of African Culture was planned there for 1962. Work by Paterson's artists had been prominent in early exhibitions and the Gallery's own group of artists was emerging

mainly at this very early stage as expressionistic painters of narrative landscapes in oils. Ned left Chirodzo in October 1961 and took over Nyarutsetso. Nyarutsetso was a very different place from Chirodzo, where Ned had an ordinary classroom for his work. Nyarutsetso was very well equipped, and it included 'two great rooms, an office, storeroom, hall and outside shelter'. Chirodzo gave Ned twenty trees as a parting gift and these went into the grounds of Nyarutsetso.

Ned's work at Nyarutsetso falls into two phases: 1961 – 65 and 1965 – 68. At first he was teaching art to some 2 000 pupils a day, all boys, aged 9 to 13 from seven, (later eight) different government primary schools. There were seven hour-long classes a day so it was full-time work. Richard Rachidi, a Malawian school-teacher trained at Cyrene (the first Malawian qualified art teacher) and Dane Chimudzi, also Cyrene trained, joined Ned as assistants. Again, painting was basic, sculpture developed later. 'Soon we had all available wall space covered with paintings in poster colour by selected pupils. All of them had drawing books and access to watercolours. In no time the scheme was in full swing with visitors coming sometimes in groups of up to 80 people'. As at Cyrene there was little formal teaching, but occasional assistance to individual pupils. 'There was no idling, the children came running to their classes and set to work immediately.' The art was communal. One boy would show his work to another and be encouraged by the cries 'Eh! Eh!' in admiration. The subject matter of the paintings ranged from scenes of rural life to scenes of violence. In 1962 political violence erupted in the townships. 'One boy showed me his bandaged thigh. "What happened?" "Police dog bit me."

"What were you doing?" "Stoning Sithole's car." "Make a picture of it." '

There was as lot of fighting among rival nationalist groups, a lot of stoning, and a lot of African houses were damaged by

Colourful posters: Ned and students at Nyarutsetso Art School, Highfields, Harare, 1963

'Mother and Child' — a study in Iroka wood by Joseph Muli done at Nyarutsetso Art Centre. (Courtesy of Ministry of Information)

'The flight to Egypt' — a sculpture in Mukwa wood done by Richard Rachid at Nyarutsetso. The height is just over two feet. (Courtesy of Ministry of Information)

George Thomson, the Commonwealth Secretary and a friend of Paterson, paying a visit to Nyarutsetso.

petrol bombs. Nyarutsetso was in the centre of it all, but was undamaged.

Violence, in war and peace, showed itself in many of their pictures — bombings, fights, burning houses, road accidents, dog fights, thefts and arrests, hunting and so on. Some boys showed interest in perspective in landscapes. Lino-cutting was done, and prints made. Ned started sculpture in wood and serpentine stone. Then, in 1963 there was a big find of soapstone, soft green steatite which can be carved with a knife, in Inyanga. The Inyanga soapstone deposits, partly developed by the sculptor Joram Mariga and Mrs Pat Pearce, an enthusiast for rural crafts, helped to move the local Africans' art from painting to sculpture. Among many other reasons for this development including African sensitivity to tactile forms, was a critical shortage of artists' paints which developed with Sanctions in 1966. Nyarutsetso carvings became very popular with tourists and souvenir dealers, unfortunately, as the tourist trade is both lucrative and unimaginative. In 1963, after the breakdown of the Federation of Rhodesia and Nyasaland, Ned was invited to join the new Board of Trustees of the National Gallery, a task which he accepted. In 1965 at the Commonwealth Arts Festival in London an exhibition of 'New Art From Rhodesia' (75 sculptures, mainly by Africans) was shown and won acclaim. By this stage McEwen's Workshop School was well into its stride, and McEwen was increasingly stressing the role of its art to express African folk-lore and proverb imagery. One dream of McEwen's however, never seriously contemplated by Ned, was the establishment of a multi-racial art centre. At the time this proved impossible, as the artistic aims of black and white were different. In 1965, Ned was asked to take mixed classes of boys and girls from the Highfield African schools, a completely new development for him. 'Almost immediately I saw, with amazement, that the aim and purpose of art in girls was utterly different from that of boys'. He had not noticed this

at exhibitions of European children's art, he believed, because the teachers had imposed their ideas on pupils of both sexes. But Nyarutsetso was different, and revealed the same sort of cultural differences that are found in popular fiction for the two sexes, advertisements, etc.

'The art of the girls is a peaceful one, in contradiction to the violence in the art of the boys: scenes of domestic life, a wedding, going to town, visitors from the city in smart clothes, household chores, work in the fields. Many include poultry, or a dog, a cat, a flower garden, even a hosepipe and tap.' Country women had to carry stream water long distances. The story goes of an African visitor to Aberdeen some years back who was asked what was the most amazing sight there. 'The pure water which comes into your homes' was the reply. There was 'a great stress on decorative landscape, trees and flowers, the pictures as it were up ended and filled in with detail, with a bosomy line of hills sometimes to mark near distance. Nearly always the human figure is static and even when doing a figure in motion it is arrested motion; a conventional pose.

Many of the girls painted the world of fashion: the gay dress, the Afro-Asian wig, the high-heeled shoes, the handbag, the little dog on a lead. Pride in their household goods showed itself in the way they made the front of the house or hut transparent so that the furniture could be seen with an array of dishes on a dresser, a vase of flowers on a cloth set askew on a table; pictures on the walls'. Ned gathered together a great hoard of the pictures of these boys and girls and circulated them to universities and art schools overseas. Turning to the relationship between art, nature, and religion Ned reflected on the beliefs that, as Hopkins put it, 'the world is charged with the grandeur of God' and that in art and agriculture man shares in God's creative work. His thoughts returned to the beloved desert of his childhood. 'Art and religion have a common root. Take the small, simple things in the Karoo, the koggelmanders (desert lizards) and the stones and bush; they are in many ways more beautiful than places like Stellenbosch,' cf Matthew 6, 24 – 34. Stellenbosch is one of the most beautiful towns in Southern Africa. The philosophy of Matthew 6:28 – 34 underlay Ned's home economics, at times to the mild consternation of his family. *Kuwadzana*, a Highfield magazine published a farewell to Ned, 'Highfield's Honorary Resident' by a former pupil (Aug/Sept, 1969). The anonymous writer notes the success of Ned's pupils in such non-art areas as History, Geography, Nature Study and Hygiene. He quotes a story of Ned's, about a drawing pupil who said to another, 'When I grow up I shall draw for my son and he'll think I am God!' Ned commented, 'These kids have learnt something they can keep till their old age.'

Paterson has helped a lot of young people find themselves and they are spread all over the country. He still keeps touch with all his former pupils. Not exactly his pet scholar because 'I couldn't draw worth a nickel,' the writer remembers Ned as gentle, patient, peaceful, sincere, understanding and intolerant of laziness. Ned has a quick and pleasant smile, and a mischievous, boyish twinkle in his eye. 'God bless him wherever he may be'.

Hence his success in turning out ordinands and lay witnesses. Ned had the same passions as other people, but chose to use them for God and man, not power or pleasure. He also encouraged people to talk about their problems and their beliefs.

Moreover Ned had passed through the long darkness of Molly's loss and shared her triumphant joy in everlasting life. This gave him a special ability to comfort the bereaved. Unafraid of death he knew it was the wrench of parting which gave pain. 'We felt he was the only one of the priests to whom we could communicate directly. Unlike the others, he didn't hide behind his dog collar.' Because he felt he had no right to judge others, this directness made him poor in the confession box.

Hearing people's problems interested him, hearing their sins embarrassed him.

Instead his bawdiness, like boisterously greeting Paget on New Year's Day with 'Happy Circumcision!' asserted the joyful unity of life. Children and young people loved him for his directness and openness, despite his own worries. One Lent about 1955, his daughter Margaret, a 17 year-old trainee nurse, picked up polio from a patient and nearly died. He brought barley-sugar to her hospital bed. A shocked little voice — 'Daddy, don't you know it's Lent?' As she approached her final crisis, in the Cathedral pulpit, erect and firm, he preached the last of a series of sermons on the Creed. His theme was The Resurrection of the Dead, and the Life of the World to come. Not a pause betrayed his anxiety. But as he finished firm and triumphant and slipped out of the church to be with her at the end, 'there was a grasp of admiration' at his unbending faith. It was as Margaret wished; the Church came first. In the event she lived on, 'a delicious person,' as Dame Molly Gibbs puts it, crippled in body but buoyant in spirit. She even outlived Ned, dying of cancer in 1976, her extraordinary spirit an example to everyone. Attempts to obtain training as a clockmaker and typewriter mechanic failed. Margaret became a receptionist with the Lion Match Company and was promptly nicknamed Our Little Lion. A very tiny but very determined person, she devoted herself to an amazing number of good works and practical hobbies, such as flower arranging. 'She was so full of interest in other people, just as Ned was, that they found themselves telling her all about their lives. She was that sort of person'. She also succeeded in driving a car — driving down alone to her twin Dugald's wedding in Johannesburg. Like Dugald, indeed, she was a bit 'car mad' and used to drive in motor rallies 'and win', says her sister Mary proudly. After her death, Fr R. 'Reg' Hambrook wrote from England, 'so the lark has risen at last!'

By the 1970s Ned had two daughters, Mary and Barbara, and a son, Dugald, safely married. Mary, after eight years cataloguing and fieldwork in the remote bush for the National Museum in Bulawayo, had married Barrie Ball, later Chief Game Warden, in 1959, and combined a roving life of adventure in the wilderness with the trials and joys of raising three young children.

Barbara, qualified as a Queen's Nurse, ended up on the island of Mull, by Scotland's Iona Abbey. Then she returned to this country and, in 1967 brought great joy to both families by marrying Nigel, world-roving son of Sir Humphrey and Dame Molly Gibbs. Sir Humphrey's very full career has of course included, among much else, farming, chairing the board of trustees for Cyrene, and bravely serving the Queen as Governor of Rhodesia during the troubled times of the 1960s — the only local Governor the colony ever had. Nigel and Barbara are now settled in a house called Cyrene in Gloucestershire. Dugald, Margaret's twin, went to Johannesburg, became an electrical engineer and married a Catholic girl. Ned was delighted, and rubbed his hands with glee at the number of future grandchildren *that* implied! Like Margaret (nicknamed Lolly because as a child he could not pronounce her name), Dugald was 'car mad'. Once he very calmly remarked 'I think you'll see something about me in today's paper' — and there, on the front page, was a picture of his car performing a triple somersault during a race.

Nicholas, Kay's only son, remained unmarried. For him, as for Margaret, God had other work. His life was short, but full of richness. Gifted like Ned with abundant health, and despite a passion for butterflies that could have made him a famous entomologist, he decided like Barbara and Margaret to give his life to the service of God and man as a doctor. His gaiety and compassion, his enthusiasm for life, mischievous laughter, and infectious grin brought happiness to the wards where he worked.

The country's first Medical Cadet, he had newly qualified and was based at Umtali (Mutare) in 1976. Margaret, his favourite sister, was near the end of her final illness in Harare. They had been very close. He came up from Mutare to visit her and was killed in a motor accident. Margaret and Nicholas are buried in Harare Cathedral cloisters, and Ned lies a couple of paces away. Ned's old friend Fr Reg Hambrook died of heart failure soon afterwards.

But this was after Ned's death, and his last years, at Farayi were, despite illness, very busy and full ones. Farayi Art Centre, Mbare Msika, was the last of Ned's many ventures in art. From his first coronary in 1965, Ned had been tired, but his explosive enthusiasm for life remained. All his stone carvers came from Nyarutsetso with him. Ned was also asked to supervise a painting centre nearby. He found it occupied by a group of souvenir painters from the Congo who had to be asked to leave. Richard Rachidi had returned to Malawi where he set up his own Art Centre. He is now said to be a successful business man in Kota Kota. Kingsley Sambo, a lively young Cyrene-trained painter and cartoonist took over as painting instructor, and Ned came to the Centre every morning from Monday to Friday to supervise, handle the money, and encourage the artists. Harry Taaka, Ned's chief sculptor, would issue the Inyanga soapstone to the artists. The stone was ordered in bulk from Inyanga, sold at cost to the sculptors, and a small commission charged on the sale of the finished works.

Fr Hambrook describes the situation in 1974: "The sculptors' yard is a hive of industry, with about thirty African young men and some boys, no more than fifteen years of age, all happily at work-dust everywhere, plus the litter of stone fragments. A transistor radio betrays its dust-camouflaged existence as it noisily fills the air with African folk music from the local radio station. A club-footed man arrives and successfully competes, armed with a flute. Ned says: 'There are a lot of Africans who can't find work, and amongst them are some who are physically incapacitated. For example, there is a blind man who reads braille. He was taught to read it at the Dutch Reformed Mission near Fort Victoria, in the African language, and he has a choir of two women and two boys and they come and sing here sometimes, and the sculptors are always very generous on such occasions, filling their little containers with cents. Also we get visits from a ventriloquist, a very fat man, who has apparently got a very recalcitrant baby in his tummy. He speaks to this baby and smacks his belly, and the baby cries and makes remarks which amuse the onlookers. Then there is the man with snakes. He is very popular, always sure of getting a crowd to watch his performance.

A municipal dust-cart, if one can call a three ton lorry such, arrives periodicially to clear up the unwanted stone fragments and does so amid clouds so thick with powdered stone that all operations come to a stand-still among the sculptors for the time being.

The visitors are frequent and they will often stand watching as if fascinated as the sculptors work. In no time a shapeless piece of stone becomes a head, then the head of an old man or a woman or a young boy. One sculptor specialises in chess sets and has a regular order, enough to keep him busy for some time. Another concentrates on animal forms, while yet another one does abstract. The finished article is pale smoky grey until treated with a coat of vegetable oil which immediately transforms its appearance by bringing out shades of colour not apparent before.'

Ned says that 'there are at least eight of these sculptors whose earnings from their work here total, for each of them, about 200 dollars a month (about £160 in English money) and about 15 000 to 20 000 dollars a year is pumped into the African economy by the Farayi Art Centre.' "

Ned himself was content with his small stipend, content to **69** have been the 'baking powder', as he put it, which stimulated the work. His own works were done for God, to decorate churches. He was content that he had not buried such talent as he possessed.

He also had the special joy of knowing that he had helped others pass on the gifts of love and service. For example, William Mariwi, whose work had been admired in 1949 by Queen Mary, visited Ned in 1973 with a pupil of his own, Captain Obiah Mutsigwa of the Salvation Army. Mariwi had become a successful storekeeper, sculptor and teacher. He had raised six children. The eldest had become a nurse and the others were all doing well. At the end of the visit, Captain Mutsigwa led the Patersons and Mariwi in a great spontaneous prayer of thanksgiving to Almighty God for the creative impulse given to man for the enlightenment of the Word, for heart, for mind and for the Holy Spirit within us. In such things Ned found a full and overflowing reward for his past pains and struggles, and new hopes for the future in this troubled land.

HUMOUR AND THOUGHT

This Harare period is the time of most of the surviving jokes about Paterson. His impish sense of humour helped to keep him young at heart and helped him to release tension. The effect of his often slanderous jokes is frequently lost in writing.

A long campaign to have his old friend Michael Gibbs made Bishop of Matabeleland was lost when Gibbs wisely withdrew and a compromise candidate Bishop Beaven was appointed.

Ned describes the arrival of the new Bishop to a welcome by the Ven. Archdeacon Hunt who opposed Gibbs, 'The Venomous Archdemon greets the Performing Bear.' The Bishop later offered Ned a job at a remote mission in Botswana, at Maun.

Often Ned's humour was a bit vulgar, and it was frequently addressed against women 'Knitting is something women do to prevent themselves thinking while they talk.' 'She would be quite attractive if only she would keep her mouth closed.' 'She is a bifurcated clothes-peg with a head missing,' etc. He liked to insinuate that public figures were guilty of minor and major improprieties, and he had a cartoonist's capacity to exaggerate. Sometimes Ned's sense of the grotesque was static, like his description of Hugh and Betty Finn, the one slender, the other pleasantly plump. 'He looks as if he had been in a famine and she as if she had caused it'. Sometimes it was more dramatic, as when he mischievously imagined a priest and a pretty girl candidate falling together into Harare Cathedral's huge baptismal font, 'the girl climbing out, the water revealing her vital statistics. It should be made into a wishing well'.

He sometimes got into strange scrapes himself, and loved telling stories about them. Once he knelt to pray by a deathbed in the Cape. There was a resounding crash as he knocked over the beer-bottles stored under the bed for the funeral. Another time he asked a lady at a party when her baby was due. In fact she was recovering from an abdominal operation.

In religion he attacked the Puseyite obsession with ritual. One story told of a priest who could only preach confession; it was his sole interest. Ordered by his Bishop to preach on St Joseph for a change, he began 'St Joseph was a carpenter who made confessional boxes'. On one television priest who seemed proud of his divine inspiration, Ned wrote 'he cocks his head as if waiting for a page of the Koran to came fluttering down and then says a windy nothing.' He believed firmly that faith is expressed in kindness to others.

One theme which turns up in many forms is the pretentiousness of clergy. He even attacked his old friend Archbishop Paget. 'The big boy condescended to come down to us in the slums. God spat at the condescension and the working man was not impressed. He should have made less noise and shared the burdens of the poor.' Of another highly paid cleric Ned acidly observed 'he hunts for God in John Haig whisky bottles.'

He felt committees and synods wasted time. 'The men who invented cheap port and committees should be impaled. Clergymen are like manure. All in a heap they stink but spread thin in the fields they do a great deal of good'. Of the community of mankind he noted that no-one is so weak that he cannot teach and help the rest of us. None is so great that we cannot help him. God has work for every single one of us. But he also sadly noted 'I saw written on a wall, ''you are never too old to learn a new stupidity.'' '

Ned's theology at this time was simple. 'Our Lord was crucified by all mankind of all time. We were there and turned the gun of selfishness and wilfulness onto Our Lord. *Each one of us* is involved in that act, just as each is able to share in His victory. The solution to our troubles and fears lies in our handing over life in every detail to Christ, to offer up our blunders, our feelings, our miseries and accept forgiveness from the Cross. The missioner's job is to suggest that faith is as simple as breathing: a handing over to Christ. And then? To get it back transformed. Religion can't be taught. It is caught, like smallpox, from the example of some Christ-centred person. It is seldom anything that he says. But his conduct reveals that he draws water from a purer well than we do' (cf John 4:14).

'You can only serve God as the individual he created. The saint is the person who sees God all the time in people, in all creation, even in a railway station, and helps others. We can only exist in relationship to others. Like Martha's Mary, our souls, which came from the perfection of God are on a pilgrimage back to Him. Our greatest desire should be to possess and be possessed by God.'

Sometimes our vision is a little dim. 'The eye specialist tells me I shall just be able to see where I am going' he wrote in

1971. 'I said, "that's wonderful, I haven't been able to see where I am going for 76 years".' 'We are just flawed windows' — so, we have reason to be modest. 'It's all right being a worm, so long as you keep a light on your tail to help others on a bit — a glow-worm!' No one group has a monopoly of wisdom, he noted. 'The walls of the denominations do not reach as far as Heaven, I don't think it matters a hoot whether a person is a (conscious) believer or not. Our Lord knows who serve him. Christ's work was not to bring God to us but us to God. It's the kind of life one lives that matters.

DEATH AND VISION

'It is just like crossing a river in flood. You wade through the peak of the flooded river and gradually come out on the other side to the sandy bank. Then you need three days' rest. After that, you are joyful and refreshed and with your Master' (Ned to Kay, Nov 16th 1974). Ned remained very active, despite a rodent ulcer and bronchial asthma, until shortly before his death. He even went to work at Farayi on Nov. 18th and spent much of Nov. 20th addressing the Christmas cards which he designed each year. Kay left for a cocktail party on the 20th, leaving Heather Fraser, an old friend, to sit with Ned. Ned collapsed and was taken to hospital. Margaret and Kay rushed there. Ned looked up, surprised to see them. 'What are you doing here in short frocks? I am going to Farayi in the morning'. Then the Dean Richard Cutts, now Bishop of the Argentine, said prayers, and Kay and Margaret kissed Ned farewell. By a twist of fate, Ned died on the feast day of St Edmund the Martyr, the only English King not named Edward to be widely revered as a saint.

Before the funeral, Kay sent off the Christmas cards, which Ned had inscribed with a quotation from the Syrian Liturgy of St. James. The cards arrived after the funeral to the bewilderment of some of the recipients. Ned would have liked that. The quotation ends 'Thou has received what was ours and given unto us what was thine'. This perhaps can stand most simply as Ned's epitaph.

A funeral was held at Harare Anglican Cathedral on November 25, 1974. The Cathedral was packed to overflowing with Neds friends of all races and backgrounds. Mrs Ellen Chudy, a Jewish friend was there. Ned had delivered the Eulogy at the funeral of her husband Morris some years before. Ned never liked a funeral to be a sad, impersonal occasion. 'He always showed care and concern for the living, for the relatives'. If a funeral could not be a joyful occasion, at least it could be a loving one. His own funeral was like that. 'It was the only funeral I've ever been to where the mourners *giggled*!'. Ellen Chudy later joined ISLAND, a voluntary group which cares for the dying and the bereaved.

Canon R.H. Clark gave the address, taking his text from the Psalm of the day of Ned's death (Ps. 104, v. 23). 'Man goeth forth to his work and to his labour until evening'. 'To attempt to sum Ned up in a few clever words would be like trying to put the ocean into a pint pot. He was artist, archaeologist, silversmith, soldier, essayist, letter-writer, will anyone collect his letters for us or would that be too dangerous while we are still alive?' (congregational laughter) 'teacher, many more and not least priest. Some 30 years ago a priest said to me, "I don't think Ned spends much time praying". And I remember my retort: "Ned prays with his hands." *Laborare est orare*: to work is to pray. I never saw Ned's hands idle until these last few years, and not often then. Always using his hands as a prayer, co-operating with the Maker of all things — painting the baldachino in Johannesburg Cathedral, whittling a piece of wood, making a fire to braai a steak, chiselling the Cyrene Font, hand-lettering the Marriage Service, enamelling the Marandellas

Cross, drawing' (even during Synod debates, in which he drew some delightfully naughty sketches of the speakers), 'feeling a piece of wood, handling a silver chalice — always using his hands. "Man goeth forth to his work and to his labour until the evening". Over the West door of the Cyrene Chapel is a mural of the Last Judgement, Cyrene style. God sits there with an adze in his right hand and a mealie cob in his left and the inscription "What have you made or what have you grown?" said the Lord as He sat on His throne." For you will not find place with empty hands." Surely, Ned will find place.'

To others, Ned's courage, dedication, overflowing compassion and humorous vitality were his key qualities, above all his readiness to help those in need at whatever cost to himself. His blunt honesty was the kind which could have made him many enemies, but combined with his love for, and interest in, everyone he met, instead it made him many friends.

Pauline Battigelli, the artist wife of the photographer Ilo the Pirate remembers Ned in his last years. 'Almost every encounter was memorable. Even a short casual call, perhaps, at his home, seemed to enliven one. As soon as I met him he reminded me of a rough-haired terrier. His vibrant little stocky body with its shock of rough hair echoed its quickness, energy and curiosity in his alert eyes. They twinkled mischievously, and the terrier was likely to bound away at any moment and return to lay something at your feet to shock you. There was a kind of glee as he registered your response to a juicy observation, or spicy bit of language, yet there was also an element of stillness in his constant watch of the human, the artistic, the precious. His hands were small and busy; open and granite; the kind of small hands that tackle huge projects. His glasses perched lightly, and he was able to shoot intimidating but wicked glances over their tops. He wore his robes, or his collar, with undisguised pride; yet he was utterly determined to be always approachable on equal ground. His jaw was square and firmly set.'

Pauline writes of his deep concern for others, even to the end — worries about the National Gallery, worries about a young doctor's unsuccessful marriage, nothing was too trivial to escape his concern, but he remained basically practical, and did not argue where it would be of no purpose. Sir Humphrey Gibbs remembers how difficult it was to argue with Ned about something he felt strongly about; without realizing how he had done it, you found yourself talking animatedly about a complete different subject, swept along by Ned's enthusiasm. 'Always his private role of helper in action continued.' Pauline also describes Ned's home: 'the whole atmosphere was one of untidy casual warmth and friendliness, treasures which were not to be locked up, but enjoyed, the old madala in the kitchen ever ready to make tea . . . creativity, the serene, smiling Mrs Kay Paterson's sterling work at social welfare steadily proceeding, Canon P. preparing an address to the Cathedral after which . . . 'down to earth again!' Nicholas, very young, very dedicated, one would guess brilliant, who had filled his room from floor to ceiling with a fascinating collection of all things of nature, leaving only room for a low bed, a table, and a small lamp . . . helpful and tolerant of his father's getting the laughs . . . Paterson had lived a full life, but seemed always to strive far more, to be digging around, nosing and unearthing, living and loving,' moved by insatiable compassion and curiosity. Mrs Battigelli particularly remembers him at sittings for his portrait, 'Sometimes one wondered if the wicked sex stories or sharp language were really coming from the man in his robes. He had lived as one with the scum of London, he'd done his bit as a rebel, as a saint perhaps — down to earth. He kept his beady eye trained on one over the top of his specs, watching for a reaction and an inward chuckle would be building up. He already had his next barrage on its way! During those portrait sittings, he sat upright, wore his regalia proudly, and swore loudly!'

Sir Athol Evans, Chairman of the Board of the National Gallery, wrote more simply, of Ned's 'wonderful sense of decency, uprightness, and determination to right any wrong and be a true friend to all'. The Right Revd Mark Wood wrote 'he taught art, life and religion at the same time, liberating people of their full potential.' Many, of all races, have written of his gift of love and power to release a sense of inner freedom. What led him on? The love of God.

'Go then alone, Thou lovely Child, in thorn-strewn wilderness, in search of Thy lost sheep. Go further still, with pierced hands and feet, to bring man back from man's disgrace, And cruelty and shame, to bring him home, Rejoicing.' (EP. 'Doggerel for Xmas, 1971', extracts).

Edward Paterson musing over two massive pieces of sculpture done by his students at Nyarutsetso. (1967)

8. *Vision*

Vision

After Ned passed on to higher service, the forty sculptors at Farayi formed themselves into a cooperative society and got permission to change their name to the Canon Paterson Craft Centre. This remains a thriving organisation, producing soft stone sculpture mainly for the tourist trade, more perhaps a comment on the market than on the artists. The writer has seen some very striking work produced by Paterson's former students, but this is usually sold privately to selected patrons who are sure to appreciate and love it. Such art, unlike tourist art, is an outpouring of the spirit, a journey of discovery, for the artist himself. The sculpture is a unique expression of his personal journey through life, and artist and patrons share that experience. Like all true art, such work is often disturbing, a bit difficult to live with. Because it is essentially honest, the truth it reveals can pain the observer, Unlike souvenir art, it requires the patron to make a decision about his outlook on life, not just about his bank balance. And unlike souvenir art, it is in a sense indestructible: it exists to make an impact on people, including the artist. The impact made, the artifact can be destroyed physically but can never be destroyed spiritually. The question it asks, the answer it suggests about man, nature, or God remain in the minds of the observers, and are reflected in their future actions. All such art is more than decoration, more than statement, more even than much prayer.

Ned saw lives like this too. 'He gave our people a sense of self-respect'. 'He amazed us with his respect for life in all its force'. 'He taught us that we should not pretend to be different, but be ourselves, and accept ourselves for what we are'. 'Other people taught us about Christ. We experienced Christ in him.' As a teacher, he saw lives as growing into a pattern of perfection — not a pattern of uniform pieces, but a kaleidoscope of different individualities, each fulfilled in its own ways in the eyes of God. So keen was he to foster this varied individuality that when one of his children took up a hobby of his in adolescence Ned would give it up. In childhood it was different — he encouraged them in his own pursuits — archaeology, sketching, collecting things — but even then he encouraged them to avoid imitating one another, to avoid sketching and collecting the same things, but to go their own ways in life.

In religion as in life, he accepted the variety of things as part of God's creation. Christian, Mohammedan and Jew all served the same Master. Sects annoyed him; 'every little doggie wants its own tree'.

He was happy to serve God wherever he was asked, including Highlands Presbyterian church and a synagogue. He was happy to have Catholic grandchildren. He accepted God on God's terms, not man's.

Because of that he was intolerant in certain ways. He abhorred indolence, waste, carelessness with other people's property especially tools, lazy thinking and prejudice and petty cruelty in any form. The richness of Cyrene and Nyarutsetso painting results from the first of these. 'Fill the page!', Ned would say, 'Fill the page!'. So the boys covered the pages of their books with strange shapes and fascinating forms in glorious colours.

And he expected them to 'Fill the page!' not only in their books but in their lives. To live life, as he himself did, fully, aware of its infinite richness — aware of its endless opportunities for adventures in discovery, love and beauty, service and religion. Though he said 'Fill the page', he did not, could not, tell them what lines, what colours to use. Each of them had to find his own way, in life as in art. Ned knew too that one could have no money, but be rich in other ways, so long as one was active with one's mind and one's hands.

The Patersons lived simply at Cyrene, on a basically sound diet of home-grown food. Ned's one great luxury was his notorious pipe. He was more or less teetotal to save money and because he felt a priest, of all people, should not seem to 'search for God in whisky bottles'. Not drinking kept him healthy and alert, physically, mentally and spiritually, though he never minded others' drinking. He lived as active a life as possible, walking wherever he could, even in old age walking to his art centres. This saved money and kept him fit and physically available for service. On foot one can stop and help people, or at least smile and chat to those in need of a word of comfort or care. These momentary chances to help people were all part of life's adventures in the search for God.

Ned laid tremendous stress on manual skills. All his children had to learn a trade. Their trade could be used to help others discover themselves. Thus Adomech Moyo and other crippled Cyrene artist teachers gave their skills to others to help them find God's creative will and love in themselves. These principles Ned's family have passed on to their children. He kept a very enquiring mind — he had a passion for reading — but reading with a practical application, not just for amusement. Ned had a deep love of nature. Any walk with him in the bush was an exciting journey of discovery, as he pointed at the details of plants and revealed the myriad secrets of insect life. Snakes

particularly charmed him. At Cyrene he paid the boys to bring snakes which he proceeded to dissect for them. Ned taught by demonstration and example. He was active, loving and gentle. His sorrows, disappointments, angers and anxieties he worked off privately through hard work, gardening, drawing caricatures, writing up his diary, walking, caring, prayer or silent communion with the Universe. He brought up his children 'on emotional blackmail'. If they had been very wicked, he 'just talked to us quietly — you felt you couldn't let him down', and as you grew up, because his love and wisdom meant a lot to you, you always asked yourself 'will I hurt Daddy'? Ned carried his own crosses. 'What would Ned think?' really mattered. He was on his way to join his Master. We knew what a privilege it was to feel near him. He knew what an honour Simon of Cyrene had unsuspecting borne.

So Ned allowed his family to accept him on their own terms. 'We always did everything together'. He guided and supported, but did not dictate. It was up to the children to find their own adventures, and to make their own ways in life. 'It is good for a child to be bored,' he said. 'If it is bored enough it will find something constructive to do.' Make plenty of activities available to them, but allow them to find out for themselves what they want to do. Let them choose how they are going to 'fill the page' of life. Encourage them to be practical and active, but do not nag them into doing things against their will. If they are given toys at all they should be things like construction kits that they can make things with, discovering the joys of creation. Encourage your children and enjoy them. They will be proud of God and of you. Such was his philosophy.

Kay Paterson was recently remarried to a vigorous artist with an enquiring mind, firm faith, and bright, mischievous eyes. Jack Garrs, sub-editor and cartoonist, is Jay Gee of the *Sunday Mail*. Ned's pupils and their families are to be found everywhere. Paterson and Patson are common first names among our African population, one tribute to Ned's indirect influence. The Canon Paterson Craft Centre in Harare still flourishes, the National Gallery goes from strength to strength, and people flock to churches decorated by Ned and his former pupils. A new generation of artists is coming forward to serve God and man. Such are Job Kekana's former students Barnabas Ndudzo and David Mutasa, two of whose sculptures stand at the door of Parliament and who designed and built the eastern plate of Heroes Acre. In their fine work is reflected Ned's artistic fire. So Ned's baking powder still does its job — his love and those of Margaret and Nicholas still work with us, though they have all gone to join the Master.

What was Ned's secret? He was a simple man. He never claimed to be different from the rest of us. Ned was proud of his parents' firm faith and their perseverance in the face of poverty. Poverty taught him to prize the true riches of life, of love, beauty and service. It taught him one can happily do without all sorts of material things like processed foods and ready-made clothes. Ned loved improvising and helping others to improvise. He would have loved Alternative Technology, making pumps from old scrap metal and things like that. He improvised in art, using kitchen knives and spoons in decorating Jo'burg Cathedral. He loved solving practical problems. He found commitment easy. He learned quickly the realities of life and death. All we are, all we have, all we can ever be and do on this earth is only lent us in momentary trust by God. Without God we can do nothing, be nothing.

All his life, all he had, all he was, Ned therefore consecrated to God through his many adventures of art, faith, and loving service. Though he has gone ahead and joined the Master, we feel his loving presence with us still.

PATERSON AND POETRY

Ned Paterson enjoyed poetry, especially poetry about nature and about religious experience. He loved Scots poetry, especially that of Burns, and, it is said, he could recite virtually the whole of the Border Ballads. He was influenced by Henri Bremond's book *Prayer and Poetry,* which he lent out widely. Poetry provides glimpses of perfection beyond us and so produces prayer. Beauty leads us to God. Paterson put together in a commonplace book a great variety of poems ranging from Celtic prayers and blessings to Japanese Haiku. His own verse seems to have been largely occasional and mostly written during his 1920s. 'Lost Lullaby' (Aug 1925) is one of the first.

'Lost Lullaby'

Sleep, sleep — my child
   For Christ's sake sleep!
Or must thy wailing yet increase my shame

Moan, moan — my child;
   Thou canst but add
Care to my grief for thoughtless sin with him.

Suck, Suck my child
   This bitter breast
And swell thy starveling limbs on lust and pain.

Drown, drown my child
   We must away
To him who knows not scorn, but love enough.

Lord, have mercy upon us!
   Christ, have mercy . . .
Lord, we come.

'Via Dolorosa'

Another chance: Lord Christ, another chance!
Lord, halts Thy lonely dragging toil
To pity me? (Poor bleeding feet).

Lord Christ! Another chance! Good Lord,
Thou knowest all things — how with me
The droning bees; Scent laden air;
Slow-circling doves; big-bellied sails
On Galilee; and sweetly clear
A shepherd's pipe; an old time song
Coarse laughter through forgiven deeds
And sleepy smile and fluttering sigh . . .
Lord Christ forgive! twas thus again
God's purest sky was deepest hell
For doleful me. Lord Christ forgive!
(Poor bleeding feet). Forgive yet once,
Forgive! — Forgive! .

'In Time of Drought' — 1925
    Morning: Prime

Striding and singing,
I vie with the birds
Who carol and fly
In withered trees,
    and hope:

The dreary earth writhes
In age premature
And looks to the dawn.
Expectant, and tense
    in hope:
She scarce feels the weight
Of two racing men —
(An old and a young)
Who run to a tomb,
    with hope!

Sext

The suffocated earth is done;
The moaning mountains lie supine;
The sun tears at his long-dead love
    most brutally
    and lustfully.

Huddled and silent, the little birds weep
In shadowless branches in murdered trees.
    No sound:
    No life:
And all a liquid fire
Cascading slow — relentlessly —
    To drown my soul
    And belch it out
    in Hell.

Evening: Evensong

His pagan glory is dying away
Brazen, with scarlet and amethyst;
And skeleton earth, with laden death
   Groans horribly,
   and heaves,
And fears for hopeless dawns
   The ghost-leaves waken,
   And eerily creep
In sapless branches
For birds that sleep.
And mourning night draws a powdery pall
Over the bleaching bones and the tears of earth.

Slowly, along the dusty road
Come two sad men whose hopeless hearts
Are cheered by the stranger who walks
Between: never suspecting
The Breaking of Bread at Emmaus.

'The Breaking Of The Drought'

Oh go to the devil!
You've nothing to me;
You've flirted and promised,
And I'm through with you. Go!

And yet . . .
That's a good cloud!
(Like a man's hand)
Clouds! can it rain?
Feel this breeze! I think she means it now,
Whispering of yearnings over seas
For me — for she's been gone so long.

   Wind ahoy!
   Where's your port?
   Somewhere South
wind, wind, I'm hoping
  What have you seen?
Baron Munchausen?
Or A. Gordon Pym
   In a boat,
   In the white?
Smell! She's seen all right. Wind, O wind,
Wast Captain Oates, with stumbling feet,
Sorrowing hands, and bursting heart.
God's gentleman! God grant him rest.
   Wind, O wind
   It's you!
   O Come
   Thank God!

   Rain! Rain! Rain!
Just see that lightning's flame
Sear sobbing earth, and rip
My God-forsaken trees all splintery.
   Smite! Tear! Blast!
Let howling bowling devils loose!
Open! you tardy gates of heaven,
And strain your hinges red with rust.
No Portia, no! you're wrong, my dear. . . .

The gentle rain? Forsooth — you mean
This ranting raving raging rain
Is mercy! Mercy heaped up
To running over, and restored
Unto my sinful, grateful breast!

You fools! You naked sons of Ham . . .
You'll catch your silly deaths of cold
  With dancing in the rain!
    Round and round
    And whirling mad.
    Stamping, jumping,
    Singing, shrieking,
    Bacchic revels
    Throbbing drums
    Pulsing wildly
    In my brain.
Half closed eyes and vanished pupils.
Shining limbs are lightning dodging.
    Mad, inviting
    Think I'll join them.
      Am I mad?
  Voetsak! you fools.

That awesome sky: such Noah saw
But did not love, as I can love:
The cataracts of heaven — near dry —
Come trickling down the aching cliffs:
The clouds of stream from drowned earth rise
As incense — skeining prayerfully:
The trellis bright -- of bouncing rain —
Has Jacob's ladder been for those
Dread angels who have smoothed my brow.

Oh the grateful clean cries
Of my cattle and sheep
And my turkeys and geese:
While my jolly old cock
Bewildered but plucky;
Assertively flapping;
Indignantly crowing
At the concert of frogs
As their din rides the air
Triumphant; discordant;
    My frogs!
  Thank God!
  Thank God.

Ned encouraged his pupils to write poetry, but only a couple of these poems found their way into the commonplace book. One, from the 1920s is on the Crucifixion, and the other from Nyarutsetso in the 1960s is on the sea.

The similarities may reflect Paterson's dominant personality, but the difference of attitudes seems significant.

'The Crucifixion'

Oh! Mighty God. Oh! Mighty God,
  Who hast the strength of many waters,
The strength of thunder and of storm
  Oh, Thou art the mighty one —
    Thou art Eternally.

You can see! Yes! He is carrying our sins
Oh that mount of Calvary.
See! Oh! He is crucified between two robbers.
Father!
Thou art Eternally.

And as Jesus looks down and sees —
Oh! Yes! He sees
His mother Mary and His loving John.
He say, 'Mother, behold thy son!
Son, behold thy Mother.'
Oh! Father!
Thou art Eternally.

Our Lord looking into the heavens
As he hangs upon the mighty Cross,
Says with a loud voice —
'My God! My God!
Why hast thou forsaken me?'
His head, yes! Jesus' head drooped
And Jesus Died.

So through all the length of days
He died a willing death
Truly, truly! Father in Heaven.
    Thou art Eternally
The Alpha and Omega.

Jeremiah Monkoe
St Cyprian's
Sophiatown
South Africa

'The Sea'

Wonderful mother of waters
    Vastly blue
All angels play upon you,
    You carry our ships,
You give us fish,
    But you always take great wages.
    You have swept men away.
    Treasures of old Kings you have taken.
Now your waters are nasty.
Full of skeletons and shells of Great monsters,
    And still you ask for more.
You have sunk great men and great ships.
    Both evil, and holy.
Sometimes you give great
    Mountains of waves,
Sometimes you give us storms
    But we still regard you as
The Holy Sea.

Chris Munatsi
Form II
Highfield

80

9. *Conclusion*

THE SIGNIFICANCE OF EDWARD GEORGE PATERSON

Ned Paterson was a man of many parts: artist, archaeologist, cartoonist, craftsman, soldier, teacher, writer, and not least priest. His achievements in soldiering and archaeology have been mentioned. As a soldier in South West Africa he did not fire a single shot in anger; but he was a pugnacious peacemaker. As an archaeologist he established at Grace Dieu the existence of the Pietersburg Stone Age Culture. His interest in archaeology flowed from, and reinforced, an interest in human culture and the dignity of man in all its forms. He was more genuinely interested in African cultures and social patterns, for example, than were many missionaries of his time. Poor himself, he respected the rough vitality of the poor he met, regardless of race or creed, for he knew from direct experience the hardships of poverty.

WRITING

Writing was important to Paterson. His most important formal writing was publicity for Cyrene during the 1940s, such as the CYRENE PAPERS. Through these cyclostyled sheets and through his mass of letters, he communicated a tremendous enthusiasm for life, for the people whom he met, those to whom he wrote, and those with whom he worked. He combined this with a mischievous disregard for pretentiousness and snobbery, and a teasing sense of humour. He loved to make fun of pompous people and church leaders, puritans and prelates. He wrote his diaries for his family and friends, sometimes circulating carbon copies. He encouraged his family to do the same, stressing freshness and spontaneity. He wrote his diaries and letters in an informal, anecdotal, witty style, bubbling with fun. His sermons, more formal, were chatty, and brought the Bible figures down to the level of the everyday market place and bus stop. Ned's verse is essentially unpolished, extended prose, written rather impetuously. He was not a profound thinker, but he had the humility to see life, record and share it, as a series of pleasant adventures, and to accept, love and rejoice in people as he found them. He took life as it came and wrote and spoke of it in an easy gossipy way which people found fun. So he might open a sermon in a borrowed church with 'when the cats away the mice can play!' and refer to the Woman of Samaria's five husbands as 'Andy Capps'.

He was often mistaken, often impatient, often intolerant, and knew it. He was saddened by pride, 'a stucco wall on a tin shanty,' by self-righteousness, by cruelty. He loved other faiths, for he loved the variety with which God shows Himself to men. He stressed the vastness of God's infinite power, love and wisdom as against the infinitesimal vision of even the greatest of men.

ART

As an artist, cartoonist and craftsman Paterson showed

imagination and enthusiasm, rather than cold planning. This could lead to his changing finished work. Thus: 'I am altering the wooden Virgin and Child which the Cathedral has paid a lot for and doesn't like because the face of the Virgin looks too much like Sr J, C.R., who is 70, fairly bearded, and a considerable tiger in her own right. I've altered it once already and am trying to make her more like her legendary age of 15.' (Diary 28.6.62) His drawing and carving have freshness but often lack a certain polish. He loved the humorous touch, the bold outline, the exaggerated feature, the characteristic, expressive pose, while he loved great art and was greatly influenced by such men as Eric Gill.

He thought, as he prayed, with his hands. He had to interact with material above all to touch it, to create with it. He felt, moreover, that art involved three partners: the artist, the material with its own special qualities and oddities, and God. All art was a process of discovery of one self, of nature, and of God.

TEACHING

This made him a good art teacher, up to a point, and enabled him to reveal and release some of the talent of the Zimbabwean people. He was enthusiastic about pupils' work, partly because he regarded painting and drawing as an adventure in self-expression and in relating to the world around one. He was intolerant of the precision of formal art training with its pre-occupations with precise observation and with delicacy of line, shading, lighting, colour balance etc. He tolerated a vast amount of poor workmanship in his pupils because the finer points of art did not really interest him, so on the whole the work produced by his pupils is more spontaneous, more per-

sonal, and less formal that that produced, for example, by Father Groeber's students at Serima Mission.

Ned encouraged his pupils to dabble with a variety of materials, including paper, wood, and as early as the 1940s, soapstone. He encouraged workmanship on the themes of nature, African society past and present, and Christian religion. He was one of the small group of European art teachers in Africa who together revealed to Europe the natural talents in art of African children. To a post-war Europe bitterly disillusioned with the power of technology, conventional religions and social theories to make men happy or compassionate, this use of art was a revelation. The West was in search of a new philosophy or set of philosophies, and found this new art from Africa very exciting. Paterson's pupils both direct and indirect have achieved considerable results. Kingsley Sambo the cartoonist, killed near Rusape in 1979 in the liberation war, is one example. His paintings were exhibited abroad. One is in the Museum of Modern Art in New York. In May 1984 the National Gallery in Harare held a Retrospective Exhibition of some 40 oils done by him. Also in 1984, Barnabas Ndudzo, a former student of Ned's protegé Job Kekana had his bronze of Mbuya Nehanda placed on permanent display at the entrance to Parliament House.

NATIONAL GALLERY

On Paterson's discovery people like Sir Stephen Courtauld and Frank McEwen of the Rhodes Centenary Gallery, now the National Gallery of Zimbabwe, were to build. Sir James McDonald of Aberdeenshire and of Bulawayo left money for a Gallery as a centre of art. Ned served for many years on the Gallery Board, as did his old friend the archivist Vivien Hiller another enthusiast of African art. Sir Stephen Courtauld saw in the arts a means to make man's marks on this beautiful country themselves beautiful. The Gallery could help hold back the forces of cheap ugliness. Sir Stephen himself created a beautiful environment in his house and gardens at La Rochelle, Penhalonga. Here he showed how art, crafts, architecture, gardening and the loveliness of the landscape could be blended to make one harmonious whole of breathtaking splendour.

Frank McEwen, the first Director of the Gallery, which opened in 1957, had been Fine Arts Officer for the British Council in Paris. He tried to bring Europeans and Africans, European art and African art, together in a common pursuit of beauty. Like Sir Stephen he was saddened by the social tensions in the country. He stressed the social make-up and values of African art. The art he fostered is often grandly monumental and based on a peace-loving folklore. This art is expressionistic, gentle and peaceful. Like Paterson McEwen stressed the natural harmony between man and nature and man's essential gentleness and tolerance. He took up the idea of a workshop, a community of artists from different families and backgrounds. Unlike Paterson he kept his community small and adult, laid stress on non-Christian themes, established marketing through commercial and national channels and kept craftsmanship separate from art. Whereas Paterson had tried to develop all the social art such as pottery and weaving. McEwen focussed his attention on painting and sculpture. He understood Public Relations and Economics and, unlike Paterson, made no use of disabled people as artists.

Two small rural communities of artists were also founded, by Tom Blomefield, a tobacco farmer at Tengenenge near Sipolilo and by McEwen at Vukutu near Inyanga (later transferred to Mr and Mrs W. Burdett-Coutts). As at Cyrene the artists had the opportunity to observe and respond to the forces of nature in a friendly atmosphere; as at the Gallery they had the advantage of maturity and an artistic environment. In both Tenge-

nenge and Vukutu, as at the Gallery, the number of artists was in effect restricted. This produced good results for the same reason as Cyrene could in its early days when art was essentially viewed as a means to rehabilitate a few disabled, handicapped or unstable people. With small numbers, individuality is quickly perceived and there is less danger of mere copying. Latterly Paterson in effect taught and encouraged a vast number of mediocre artists, against his own belief that true artistic ability is confined to a tiny minority. There were one or two outstanding artists who usually were disabled like Job Kekana, Adomech Moyo and Sam Songo. For the rest Ned saw art as a form of self-expression, a means to decorate their homes, and a constructive alternative to boozing; something cheap, exciting, which keeps the men at home, out of mischief, and respected by their children. His daddy drew cats for him. He drew for his own children and encouraged them to draw. He felt art could help keep families together and keep the men away from beer and brothels. It had a social function separate from its aesthetic merit.

McEwen, by contrast, created an environment conducive to the evolution of a small number of artists of international standing and ensured the recognition of their individual talents, though the work often appeared repetitive. A McEwen exhibition stressed the talents of the individual artist and the achievement of the Workshop School as a whole. A Cyrene exhibition stressed the potential talents of African children in general and the achievements in education of S.P.G. in Africa, though Paterson encouraged talented individuals and fostered self-expression. Children went to Cyrene exhibitions for inspiration; a lot of Cyrene publicity is anti-personality cult, for Paterson wanted to encourage wide self-expression through cheap materials. Unlike McEwen, moreover, Paterson stressed the essential impermanence of art. He was basically uninterested in producing works for permanent display or commercial sale.

Paterson was more concerned with developing talents than in the production of finished works of art. McEwen by contrast took a collector's interest in the production and possession of fine sculpture. McEwen also stressed finishing processes, such as the polishing of serpentine pieces over several days, which made fine exhibition pieces but did not develop the artist's imaginative ability so readily.

In his own work and that of his pupils Paterson was more concerned to develop versatility than patient perfection in single skills though he encouraged the meticulous detail of the Cyrene painters. He also suffered from critical shortages of valuable materials. Art, for him, should be fun, not toil, and done for personal and social good, not for money.

COMMUNITY SELF-HELP

In Cyrene, Chirodzo, Nyarutsetso and Farayi, as in his own family, Paterson tried to produce communities of responsible, self-fulfilled people who were mature, independent and affectionate; people who like himself loved life, beauty, adventure, nature, other people in all their variety and God. He stressed the principles of mutual help and the dignity of manual work. As Nicky (aged 4) put it when asked what God made whales of, 'it doesn't matter: it's the hands that count.' Paterson stressed the need to work for one's community and in Highfield he was a driving force behind the weaving centre and the Public Library. Reading, like manual work, should be practical and fun. He had learned that back in Noupoort, where Bunting-Smith had encouraged the senior pupils to discover the adventure of reading for themselves in the local Library. Paterson had no time for people, regardless of race, creed or outlook, who exploited others and used political or social power to serve themselves and not mankind.

GUIDING LIGHT

Ned saw that man without a religious vision, without the God of Love, would always make a hash of life. He worked at love with enthusiasm, patience, and affectionate thanksgiving for mankind despite our flaws. He laughed a lot at our abilty to take our pride, our fantasies of wealth, love and power, to church with us and to dress them up in pretty phrases and comic postures.

Action, not words, not pretty formulae, are what count. So Ned found God's living presence under many faiths and sects, wherever men love mankind and look for God (Matt. 7:7). The Christ he served was God indeed, but set a standard of leadership in simple dress and ways. This Christ spoke to all, 'each in his own language' (Acts 2.6), even imprecise, uncouth Aramaic or slum slang. This Christ was shown in love and loving deeds and laughter. Through the home, the family, the club, the school, He could reach out and spread a little light and joy; even by letters, pictures and the printed page.

Ned saw ALL human actions done for God in others as creative art — even dusting a room. All life is art. All art in a material sense is impermanent, subject to change and decay. It is not our job to be Marthas, building God's Kingdom on earth, but Marys, finding Him. All unselfish acts are works of art and permanent. They exist for ever in the Mind of God. Art is everything done for God in mankind. By each unselfish act we let ourselves be changed, partners with God who creatively works within us. At last, the dull clay of our earthly frame forgotten we may, like our love, come to exist forever united in the Mind of God. God is the one Creator and the first and final Artist. He is the Beginning and the End. His Kingdom is the one creation of all things.

All our lifetime we are free to choose the Adventure of Loving Faith, the one true Art, or to bury our talent in the dusty ground. We must not delay. We cannot leave the decision to God alone. That Artist has already chosen for us. He has brought us the gift of Eternal Life. He is knocking patiently at the doors of our hearts. Don't you hear Him? The only door handles are on our side. Have we the love, the vision, the courage and the sense of adventure to open the door? Shall we let Him in?

Gweru
Advent
1984

SELECTED LIST OF WORKS CONSULTED

Arnold, Marion. *Zimbabwean Stone Sculpture*. Bulawayo, Books of Zimbabwe, 1981.

Brémond, Henri. *Prayer and Poetry*. London, Burns & Oates, 1927.

Brown, Evelyn, ed. *Africa's Contemporary Art and Artists*. New York, Harmon Foundation, 1966.

Carline, Richard. *Draw They Must*. London, Edward Arnold. 1968.

ffrench-Beytagh, Gonville. *Encountering Darkness*. London, Collins, 1973.

Gibbon, Geoffrey. *Paget of Rhodesia*. Bulawayo, Books of Zimbabwe, 1973.

Humphriss, Deryck and Thomas, D.G. *Benoni*. Benoni, Benoni Town Council, 1968.

Jenkins, David and Stebbing, Dorothy. *They Led the Way*. Cape Town and Harare, Oxford University Press, 1966.

Kuhn, Joy. *Myth and Magic*. Cape Town, Don Nelson, 1978.

Morgan, E.R., and Lloyd, R., eds. *The Mission of the Anglican Communion*. London, SPCK and SPG, 1948.

Mount, Marshall Ward. *African Art: The Years Since 1920*. Bloomington, Indiana University Press, 1973.

Paterson, E.G., *The Cyrene Papers*. Cyrene Mission, 1940 – 53 (cyclostyled).

Plangger, A.B., and Diethelm, M. eds. *Serima: Towards an African Expression of Christian Belief*. Gweru, Mambo Press, 1977.

Rosenthal, Eric, ed. *Encyclopaedia of Southern Africa*. London, Warne 1961.

Scott, G.M. *A Time to Speak*. London, Faber and Faber — 1958.

Thomson, Doris. *Priest and Pioneer, a memoir of Osmund Victor. C.R.* London, The Faith Press. 1958.

Wall, Barbara. 'Canon Paterson of Cyrene' in *Arts Zimbabwe, No 2* (1981 – 2) pp 27 – 38. Harare, National Arts Foundation. 1982.

Wood, Patricia. 'Rhodesian Art, a General Survey' in *Arts Rhodesia, No 1*, pp 3 – 19. Harare, National Arts Foundation. 1978.

Myers, B. and Copplestone, T., eds. *The Macmillan Encyclopaedia of Art*. London, Macmillan. 1977.

Aside from the rather disappointing little collection of Cyrene Art at the National Archives in Harare, the main institutionally held deposits are at USPG headquarters in London (United Society for the Propagation of the Gospel), the Central School of Arts and Crafts in London, and the Smithsonian Institute in Washington D.C., USA. Most of the rest is in private hands.   D.W.